CONFIDENT LEADERSHIP FOR WOMEN

7 ESSENTIAL LEADERSHIP SKILLS TO BUILD AUTHORITY WITH AUTHENTICITY, OVERCOME IMPOSTER SYNDROME, CULTIVATE TRUST, AND LEAD WITH IMPACT

AMBER PRESTON

To my dearest friend, whose strength and heart have always inspired me to aim higher. Your wisdom and integrity have shaped not just my journey, but the journeys of everyone lucky enough to know her. Your leadership is a beacon of courage, compassion, and commitment, and I am endlessly grateful for you. PS, I love you.

CONTENTS

INTRODUCTION

As I sat in a conference room full of seasoned executives, I felt a knot of doubt tightening in my stomach. I was the only woman at the table, and I was about to present a major project proposal. My mind raced with questions: Would they take me seriously? Did I really belong here? In that moment, I also realized how often I had let these doubts hold me back. After the meeting, which went better than I had feared, I knew I had to address these barriers. Not just for myself, but for other women facing the same challenges. This realization planted the seed for this book.

At its core, this book is about empowerment. It aims to help female leaders build authority and overcome challenges in environments that may not always welcome them. It's about shedding the masks we wear and being true to ourselves, while still achieving great things.

Women in leadership roles often face unique hurdles. Gender biases can skew perceptions. Imposter syndrome can undermine confidence. According to recent studies, women are still underrepresented in top leadership positions. This gap highlights the importance of strategies that empower women to lead authentically and effectively.

Many leadership books offer abstract theories. This book offers seven pivotal skills with concrete steps you can take, starting today. Each chapter will dive deep into each skill, providing practical tools and insights. It includes diverse success stories, showing that there is no single path to effective leadership. This diversity reflects the varied experiences of women in leadership and provides a wide range of relatable insights. These stories, coupled with data-driven insights, will provide a robust framework for each skill.

Whether you are stepping into a leadership role for the first time or seeking to refine your approach, I hope this book offers tools and brings inspiration. The path to impactful leadership is not a solo journey. It is a shared adventure. Together, we will explore the skills that empower you to lead with confidence and authenticity. The journey awaits, and I am thrilled to walk it with you.

SKILL #1 - EMBRACING AUTHENTIC LEADERSHIP

I t was a typical Tuesday morning, yet something felt different. As I prepared for a leadership meeting, I couldn't shake off the feeling that I was wearing a mask. I was about to discuss strategic plans with my team, but internally, I was wrestling with the dissonance between the leader I thought I should be and the person I truly was. At that moment, it hit me: the most effective leaders I knew were those who led with authenticity. They were unapologetically themselves, and their teams thrived because of it. This realization set me on a path to explore what authentic leadership really meant. This chapter is about sharing that discovery with you, so you can lead in a way that feels genuine and powerful.

1.1 DISCOVERING YOUR AUTHENTIC LEADERSHIP STYLE

To lead authentically, you must first understand what authenticity means for you. This requires deep reflection on your core values and beliefs. These are the principles that guide your decisions and actions, even when no one is watching. Take a moment to consider what truly matters to you. Are there values you hold close, such as integrity, empathy, or innovation? Reflecting on these can provide clarity. Try a personal reflection exercise where you jot down moments when you felt most aligned with these values. This exercise will help you identify patterns and insights into your authentic self.

Once you have a grasp on your values, it's time to explore your unique leadership strengths. Each of us possesses distinct qualities that set us apart. Perhaps you are a natural communicator, or maybe your strength lies in strategic thinking. Identifying these strengths can be eye-opening. Consider taking a strengths-finding assessment to uncover these attributes. These assessments can highlight traits you might not even be aware of, offering a fresh perspective on your capabilities. Remember, authentic leadership is not about mimicking others; it's about embracing what makes you uniquely you.

With your values and strengths in mind, the next step is to create a personal leadership vision. This vision acts as a guiding star, aligning your actions with your authentic self. Crafting this vision involves envisioning the impact you want to have as a leader. What legacy do you wish to leave? Use vision statement templates to articulate this clearly. A well-defined vision not only motivates you, but also inspires those you lead by providing a sense of purpose and direction.

Developing self-awareness is crucial in this journey of authentic leadership. Understanding how your personal traits influence your style helps you lead more effectively. Engage in journaling prompts for self-discovery to enhance this awareness. Write about your reactions to different situations, your emotions, and how these impact your leadership. This practice can be revealing, uncovering subconscious patterns that shape your interactions. As you gain self-awareness, you will notice an improvement in how you manage your team and make decisions.

In this process of discovering your authentic leadership style, remember that authenticity is not a destination but a continuous exploration. As you grow and evolve, so will your understanding of yourself. Embrace the journey with openness and curiosity, knowing that your authenticity will empower you to lead with impact and purpose. This chapter sets the stage for you to step into your authentic power, equipping you with the tools to lead confidently and effectively in any environment.

1.2 BUILDING CONFIDENCE THROUGH AUTHENTICITY

Confidence and authenticity are intertwined in leadership. When you embrace your true self, you naturally project confidence. Think of leaders like Indra Nooyi, Former Chief Executive Officer of PepsiCo, who emphasize empathy and self-awareness. Their success stems from authenticity. When you lead from a place of honesty, your confidence is genuine, not an act. People can sense this. Authentic leaders don't have to pretend or put on a mask, which is liberating. When you accept and express your true self, you free up energy to focus on leading with assurance and conviction, rather than worrying about maintaining a facade.

Fear of vulnerability often holds people back from authenticity. Many leaders worry that showing vulnerability will expose them to judgment. However, vulnerability can actually be a powerful leader-ship tool. Consider the example of Beth Jannery, who emphasizes vulnerability as a leadership strength. When you're open about your challenges, you create a space for others to do the same. This open-ness fosters trust and deepens connections. I recall a time when I admitted uncertainty during a project. Instead of losing respect, I gained it. My team appreciated the honesty and rallied to support the project more vigorously, knowing they were part of a genuine dialogue, not a one-sided directive.

Self-acceptance plays a crucial role in building confidence through authenticity. It's about acknowledging imperfections and recognizing them as part of your unique leadership style. The path to self-acceptance can be challenging.

Interactive Exercise: Working Towards Self-Acceptance

Initiate your journey towards self-acceptance with self-compassion by engaging in this daily exercise designed to enhance your appreciation for yourself. Each morning or night, write down three things you appreciate or value about yourself. This could range from professional accomplishments to personal virtues such as kindness or resilience. Over time, this reflective practice naturally redirects your attention away from your perceived shortcomings and towards a more positive recognition of the innate strengths and capabilities you bring to your leadership role.

Authenticity also enhances decision-making. When you lead authentically, you make decisions that align with your true values and beliefs. This clarity results in more decisive and impactful actions. Imagine a scenario where you face a difficult choice between two potential business strategies. An authentic leader, grounded in their values, will choose the path that reflects their core principles, even if it's the more challenging option. This alignment with personal values creates a sense of purpose and determination that enhances decision-making. Trust yourself to make decisions that are true to who you are, rather than trying to fit into a mold that doesn't suit you.

Incorporating authenticity into leadership isn't about following a set formula. It's about finding what works for you and embracing it fully. As you do, you'll find that your confidence grows naturally. You'll stand firm in your decisions, not because you're following someone else's lead, but because you're following your own. Authenticity is the foundation upon which true confidence is built, empowering you to lead with strength and integrity.

1.3 BALANCING ASSERTIVENESS WITH EMPATHY

Assertiveness and empathy might seem like two opposing traits, but they are not only compatible; they are essential partners in effective leadership. Assertiveness involves expressing one's thoughts and needs clearly and confidently, without aggression. It means standing firm in your decisions and positions while respecting others. Empathy, on the other hand, involves understanding and sharing the feelings of others. It's about seeing the world through someone else's eyes and responding with compassion. Together, these traits create a balanced leadership style that respects both the leader's and the team's perspectives, fostering an environment of mutual respect and collaboration.

Effective communication is the cornerstone of harmonizing assertiveness with empathy in leadership. One powerful strategy is the use of "I" statements. This technique involves framing your thoughts and feelings from your own perspective, minimizing the risk of coming across as accusatory. For instance, articulating concerns like, "I feel frustrated when deadlines are missed, as it disrupts our project's schedule," combines assertiveness with sensitivity. It signals your commitment to project timelines while considering the collective impact, encouraging a constructive dialogue rather than blame.

Additionally, integrating active listening exercises into your leadership practice is invaluable. Active listening transcends mere hearing; it requires full engagement with the speaker, an effort to truly comprehend their message, and give a thoughtful response. This method enhances the quality of communication and cements trust within the team by validating their contributions and signaling that their viewpoints are appreciated and crucial to decision-making processes. Cultivating this skill bridges gaps between team members and reinforces a culture of mutual respect and inclusivity, pivotal for nurturing a collaborative and high-performing team.

Developing emotional intelligence is another crucial step in balancing assertiveness with empathy. Emotional intelligence, or EQ, involves being aware of and managing your own emotions, as well as understanding and influencing the emotions of others. It helps leaders navigate complex interpersonal dynamics and make informed decisions. Consider using EQ assessment tools like the Emotional and Social Competency Inventory (ESCI) to evaluate your strengths and areas for growth. These tools can provide insight into your emotional processes, helping you respond more effectively in leadership roles. High emotional intelligence allows leaders to adapt their communication style and approach based on the needs of their team, maintaining a balance between firmness and understanding.

Libby Rothschild, a successful entrepreneur, is known for her assertive communication style, which she balances with deep empathy for her team. Her leadership journey shows the power of assertive clarity in setting expectations and boundaries, coupled with a profound understanding of her team's perspectives and emotional needs. She emphasizes the importance of supporting other women in leadership, aiming to eliminate gender disparities by advocating for a workplace culture that values collaboration, equity, and mutual respect. Through her actions and initiatives, Rothschild advances her organization's objectives and paves the way for more equitable leadership landscapes.

Reflection Exercise: Refining Your Communication Style

To incorporate these traits into your leadership approach, start by reflecting on your current communication style. Identifying these nuances in your communication style will illuminate pathways for integrating a balanced dose of assertiveness and empathy. Think through these questions:

- Are there areas where you could be more assertive or empathetic?

- In what situations do you find your voice firm, and where does it falter?
- Are there moments when your empathy overshadows your assertiveness, or vice versa?

Another activity you may consider is conducting role-playing exercises with trusted colleagues, where you practice scenarios that require both traits. This method allows you to receive feedback and refine your approach in a supportive environment. Additionally, seek feedback from your team regularly. Understanding how others perceive your leadership style can provide valuable insights and opportunities for growth.

Remember, balancing assertiveness with empathy is not about achieving perfection, but about striving for harmony in leadership interactions. As you explore these concepts, you'll find that this balance enhances your effectiveness as a leader and enriches the relationships within your team.

1.4 LEADING WITH VALUES AND INTEGRITY

When I think about leadership, the first thought that comes to mind is the importance of values. They form the backbone of ethical leadership, guiding every decision and action. In today's world, where leaders face ethical dilemmas with increasing frequency, having a strong value system is crucial. Imagine a leader faced with a decision that could boost profits at the cost of employee well-being. A value-driven leader would prioritize the latter, understanding that long-term success hinges on the well-being of their team. This kind of leadership fosters trust and results in loyalty among team members, who feel valued and respected.

Case studies of value-driven leadership demonstrate how leaders who anchor their actions in values inspire others and drive success. Consider the example of Nelson Mandela, whose leadership was rooted in values of equality and justice. Despite immense pressure, he remained steadfast in his commitment to these principles, earning respect and admiration worldwide. His leadership reminds us that integrity is not about choosing the easy path; it's about choosing the right one. Mandela's approach demonstrates that when leaders align their decisions with their core values, they can navigate complex situations with clarity and purpose.

Promoting ethical decision-making is a cornerstone of leading with integrity. It involves ensuring that every decision aligns with both personal and organizational values. This can sometimes lead to difficult choices, but it also sets a standard for others to follow. Ethical dilemmas often arise unexpectedly, requiring leaders to act quickly and thoughtfully.

Embedding integrity within the team and organizational culture is a continuous process. It requires leaders to create environments where ethical behavior is expected and recognized. One effective way to foster this culture is through team-building activities focused on values. These activities encourage open dialogue about what integrity means in practice, allowing team members to share their perspectives and experiences. This promotes a shared understanding of values and strengthens the team's commitment to ethical behavior. When integrity becomes ingrained in the culture, it naturally influences everyday actions and decisions.

The impact of value-based leadership is significant and far-reaching. Organizations led by such leaders often enjoy higher levels of employee engagement, customer satisfaction, and overall success. Success stories from various industries highlight how leading with values transforms teams and organizations. Companies that prioritize integrity tend to attract talent that shares similar values, creating a cohesive and motivated workforce. This alignment between personal and organizational values fosters a sense of belonging and purpose among employees, driving innovation and performance.

In the ever-evolving landscape of leadership, anchoring decisions and actions in values and integrity is not just beneficial; it is imperative. It builds a foundation of trust, fosters a positive organizational culture, and ultimately leads to sustained success. As leaders, the challenge is to consistently uphold these principles, even when faced with adversity. By doing so, we enhance our own leadership and inspire those around us to do the same.

1.5 NAVIGATING PROFESSIONAL IDENTITY WITH AUTHENTIC LEADERSHIP

Understanding professional identity is pivotal in defining how you show up in the world as a leader. It encompasses your roles, skills, values, and the unique attributes you bring to your professional environment. This identity shapes your leadership style and influences how others perceive you. It's not just about the job title you hold or the tasks you perform. Instead, it's a composite of your experiences, beliefs, and the way you choose to interact with others in the workplace. Your professional identity acts as a bridge between your personal beliefs and your role as a leader, guiding your actions and interactions.

Aligning your personal beliefs with your professional roles can create a powerful leadership style. This alignment ensures that your decisions and actions are consistent and genuine, developing trust among your team. To achieve this alignment, consider engaging in exercises that help you reflect on both your personal and professional lives. For instance, you might list your core values and then assess how these are reflected in your daily work activities. This exercise can reveal gaps or synergies, providing insights into areas where alignment can be improved or celebrated.

Adapting your identity within diverse environments requires a delicate balance between maintaining authenticity and embracing flexibility. Workplace cultures can vary widely, and what works in one environment might not suit another. As a leader, it's crucial to remain true to your core identity while being open to adjusting your approach to fit different contexts. This flexibility doesn't mean compromising your values but rather adapting your style to engage effectively with diverse teams. Consider scenarios like leading a team in a new country or industry. Each setting demands unique cultural sensitivities and leadership styles. By being open to learning from these environments, you can enhance your effectiveness while staying true to who you are.

There are many benefits to a cohesive and authentic professional identity. When you lead with consistency and authenticity, you naturally build trust and credibility. Your team knows what to expect from you and can rely on your integrity and transparency. This trust is foundational for effective leadership, as it encourages open communication and collaboration. Teams are more likely to engage and innovate when they feel their leader is genuine and trustworthy. Moreover, a consistent professional identity strengthens your reputation in the broader professional community, opening doors to new opportunities and collaborations.

Navigating professional identity with authenticity means being intentional about how you integrate your personal and professional selves. It's about recognizing that leadership is not just a role you play at work, but an extension of who you are. This cohesive identity enhances your effectiveness as a leader and enriches your experience and satisfaction in your professional life. As you continue to develop and refine your professional identity, remember that it's an ongoing process of growth and reflection, adapting as you evolve and encounter new challenges.

1.6 LEVERAGING AUTHENTICITY TO BUILD AUTHORITY

As we wrap up this chapter, you have likely realized how authenticity is a powerful tool in the realm of leadership, serving as the foundation for establishing credibility and authority. When leaders are authentic, they naturally gain trust, which is a direct result of consistently aligning actions with genuine beliefs and values. Consider leaders who openly share their challenges and learning experiences. By doing so, they humanize themselves and demonstrate transparency and integrity. This openness invites others to engage with them on a deeper level, fostering a sense of reliability and trustworthiness that is essential for effective leadership.

Authentic storytelling is a particularly effective method to convey sincerity and foster connection. It involves sharing personal anecdotes and experiences that resonate with audiences, creating a narrative that is both relatable and impactful. For instance, a leader might recount a pivotal career moment that taught them a valuable lesson. This provides context for their decisions and illustrates their journey, making their leadership style more understandable and relatable. Authentic communication goes beyond words; it requires consistent actions that reflect the values and messages being conveyed. This consistency reinforces trust and ensures that the leader's authority is grounded in authenticity.

Long-term leadership strategies rooted in authenticity often focus on empowering others, promoting collaboration, and fostering an inclusive environment. This approach encourages team members to take ownership of their roles, leading to a more engaged and motivated workforce. Leaders who prioritize authenticity in their strategic planning often find that their influence endures, as they have built a legacy of trust and respect that transcends individual projects or initiatives.

Leaders can inspire their teams by modeling authentic behavior and providing opportunities for team members to explore their own authenticity. Workshops and team exercises focused on authenticity can be instrumental in this process. These activities can help individuals reflect on their values, share their perspectives, and engage in meaningful dialogue about what authenticity means to them. Such initiatives strengthen team cohesion and empower individuals to bring their true selves to their work, enhancing overall team performance and satisfaction.

In embracing authenticity as a cornerstone of leadership, leaders create a dynamic where authority is earned thorough genuine connection and mutual respect, rather than imposed through title or position. This approach fosters an environment where individuals feel valued and understood, leading to increased collaboration, innovation, and success. By weaving authenticity into the fabric of their leadership style, leaders enhance their own effectiveness and inspire those around them to lead with integrity and purpose. As we continue to explore the multifaceted aspects of leadership, it becomes clear that authenticity is not just a leadership tool—it is a fundamental component of impactful and meaningful leadership.

SKILL #2 - OVERCOMING IMPOSTER SYNDROME

I remember standing in front of a packed auditorium, the spotlight glaring down on me, and feeling an overwhelming sense of self-doubt. Despite years of experience and countless hours of preparation, a voice inside whispered, "What if they find out you don't know what you're doing?" This nagging feeling of inadequacy, despite evidence to the contrary, is what many of us know as imposter syndrome. It's a phenomenon that affects even the most accomplished individuals, often making them feel like frauds in their own success stories. While imposter syndrome can affect anyone, it's particularly prevalent among women in leadership roles, where societal pressures and expectations can amplify these feelings. Understanding this syndrome is the first step toward overcoming it.

2.1 DEFINING IMPOSTER SYNDROME

Imposter syndrome, which could also be referred to as imposter phenomenon or fraud syndrome was first described in 1978 by Suzanne Imes, Ph.D. and Pauline Rose Clance, Ph.D. as an observation among successful women and other marginalized groups.

Clance, et al. characterized imposter syndrome by six traits: the imposter cycle, perfectionism, super-heroism, atychiphobia (fear of failure), denial of competence, and achiemephobia (fear of success). Imposter syndrome is more than just self-doubt. It's a persistent feeling of not being "good enough," coupled with the fear of being exposed as a fraud, even when achievements clearly speak for themselves. Common examples include attributing success to luck rather than skill, perfectionism that leads to burnout, and a sense of over-preparation or procrastination in tasks. This cycle of self-doubt can trap even the most capable leaders, affecting their performance and well-being.

The roots of imposter syndrome often lie in deeper psychological and societal causes. Cultural and gender norms can play a significant role in shaping feelings of inadequacy. From a young age, many women receive messages that success must be earned through perfection, leading to unattainable standards. These societal pressures can contribute to the denial of competence and the belief that success is due to external factors, rather than personal effort and skill. Understanding these underlying causes can help dismantle the internalized beliefs that fuel imposter syndrome. You are not alone in this struggle, and it's important to recognize that these feelings are often shaped by external influences beyond your control.

Creating awareness is a powerful tool in overcoming imposter syndrome. These are specific situations or thoughts that set off feelings of inadequacy. For many, performance reviews can be a trigger, as they involve scrutiny and judgment. Public speaking is another common trigger, where the fear of being judged harshly can overshadow the moment. Understanding your specific triggers can empower you to prepare for them. Reflect on past experiences and identify patterns. When do these feelings arise? What situations seem to bring them to the surface? By pinpointing these triggers, you can begin to address them proactively, rather than reacting to them.

Journaling Exercise: Understanding Your Triggers

- Reflect on a recent situation where you felt like an imposter. What were the circumstances?
- Identify any specific thoughts or beliefs that triggered these feelings. Were they related to external judgments or internal expectations?
- Consider how cultural or societal norms may have influenced your perception of competence in this situation.
- Write about a time you successfully overcame a similar challenge. What strategies did you use, and how can they apply now?

Journaling serves as an effective method for tracking and under-standing your triggers. By consistently writing down thoughts and experiences, you can gain insights into the patterns and beliefs that underlie these feelings. Journaling also encourages introspection and can reveal recurring themes in your thinking. Through this reflective practice, you can transform imposter syndrome from an over-whelming barrier into an opportunity for growth and self-aware-ness. By understanding and addressing your triggers, you empower yourself to lead with confidence and integrity.

2.2 REFRAMING SELF-PERCEPTION FOR GROWTH

Negative self-talk is a formidable challenge many of us face, particu-larly in leadership roles where the stakes are high. These internal dialogues often whisper doubts and fears, questioning our abilities and worth. To counteract this, cognitive restructuring becomes an invaluable tool. It involves identifying these negative thoughts and consciously reshaping them into positive, constructive beliefs. For instance, instead of thinking, "I'm not qualified for this task," you might reframe it as, "I have the skills and determination to succeed." This might seem simple, but it requires practice and conscious effort to change entrenched thought patterns. By consistently challenging these thoughts, you can dismantle the barriers they create, replacing them with empowering affirmations that bolster your confidence and competence.

Embracing a growth mindset is another powerful way to reframe self-perception. This mindset, defined by psychologist Carol Dweck, is rooted in the belief that abilities and intelligence can be developed through effort and learning. Viewing challenges as opportunities for growth, rather than threats to competence, allows you to see failure as a stepping stone rather than a dead end. Consider the story of Sara Blakely, founder of Spanx, who frequently shares how her father encouraged her to embrace failure as part of learning. This perspective enabled her to take risks without fear of inadequacy. By adopting a growth mindset, you cultivate resilience and openness to learning, which are crucial for personal and professional development.

Visualization is another technique that can reshape self-perception and enhance confidence. Visualization involves creating a mental image of success, immersing yourself in the feelings and experiences of achieving your goals. It's a practice used by athletes and leaders alike to enhance performance and prepare for challenges. Picture yourself confidently addressing a room full of colleagues or successfully navigating a challenging project. This mental rehearsal helps build familiarity and confidence, reducing anxiety and boosting self-assurance. Guided visualization exercises can assist in this process, offering structured paths to explore and reinforce positive outcomes. Over time, these visualizations can become powerful motivators, transforming your perceptions of what is possible.

Incorporating affirmations into daily routines can further reinforce a positive self-view. Affirmations are short, powerful statements that affirm your strengths and capabilities, helping to counteract negative self-talk. They serve as reminders of your value and potential.

For example, you might start your day with affirmations like, "I am capable and confident," or "I bring unique strengths to my team." Repeating these regularly helps internalize them, gradually shifting your mindset towards positivity and self-assurance. This practice, while simple, can have profound effects on how you perceive yourself and your abilities, setting a foundation for sustained confidence and growth.

Through these various techniques, you can begin to reshape your self-perception, challenging the doubts that fuel imposter syndrome and building a more resilient, empowered self. By actively engaging in cognitive restructuring, cultivating a growth mindset, visualizing success, and using affirmations, you create a toolkit that supports continuous personal development. These practices empower you to face challenges with confidence, viewing them as opportunities to continuously learn and grow. As you integrate these approaches into your leadership journey, they will become second nature, enhancing your self-awareness and fortifying your leadership presence.

2.3 BUILDING RESILIENCE AGAINST SELF-DOUBT

In the quiet moments of leadership, when the office is still and the day's challenges linger in your mind, self-doubt can creep in like an uninvited guest. Building resilience against this self-doubt is not just about pushing it away, but about strengthening your emotional core to withstand its whispers. Emotional resilience is your ability to adapt to stress and adversity, and strengthening it involves cultivating practices that enhance your mental well-being. Mindfulness and meditation are powerful tools here. They encourage you to remain present, acknowledging thoughts without judgment. By practicing mindfulness, you learn to observe self-doubt without letting it take root. Meditation, even for a few minutes daily, can create a space where your mind learns to pause, reflect, and respond rather than react. Over time, these practices enhance your ability to navigate challenges with a clearer, calmer mindset, allowing you to focus on solutions rather than being overwhelmed by doubts.

Daily Mindfulness and Meditation Practices

Establishing a regular mindfulness practice is key, and it can look different for everyone. The following exercises can take just a few minutes a day or longer, depending on your preferences and schedule. Just a few minutes a day can make a profound difference over time.

- Tune into your breathing. Feel your belly rise and fall with each breath.
- Do a body scan. Slowly scan your body from head to toe, noticing sensations.
- If taking a mindful nature walks, focus your senses on sights, sounds, and smells.
- Repeat your affirmations of choice, like "I am confidence. I inspire those around me. I am proud of my accomplishments."
- Observe your thoughts as they arise and pass through your mind. Acknowledge them without judgment or attachment.

Coping strategies for real-time management of self-doubt are also essential for leaders who face high-pressure situations regularly. Breathing exercises offer a simple, yet effective method for managing stress. When you find yourself in a tense situation, such as before a crucial presentation, take a moment to engage in deep breathing. Inhale slowly through your nose, hold for a few seconds, and exhale through your mouth. This technique calms the nervous system, reducing anxiety and clearing the mental fog that self-doubt creates. Additionally, developing positive self-dialogue scripts can be transformative. Prepare phrases that affirm your capabilities, such as, "I am prepared and capable to handle this presentation." Repeat these affirmations when doubt surfaces, replacing negative thoughts with empowering ones. This practice shifts your focus and reinforces a positive self-image over time.

Seeking constructive feedback is another vital strategy for overcoming self-doubt. While it might seem daunting to seek opinions when you're already questioning your abilities, feedback is a valuable mirror that reflects both strengths and areas for improvement. Engage in feedback loops with trusted colleagues who understand your work and support your growth. Invite them to share their observations, focusing on constructive insights that can guide your development. This process provides clarity and helps you see beyond your self-imposed limitations. When received with an open mind, feedback empowers you to make informed decisions about your leadership journey. It also fosters a culture of openness and learning, encouraging others to seek and provide feedback constructively.

The pursuit of progress over perfection is a mindset shift that liberates you from the paralyzing grip of perfectionism. Many leaders fall into the trap of setting unattainable standards for themselves, believing that anything less than perfect is inadequate. However, this mindset can lead to burnout and dissatisfaction. Instead, focus on incremental growth and celebrate small victories along the way. Use goal-setting frameworks that emphasize progress. Break larger goals into manageable steps, and acknowledge each completed task as a milestone. This approach not only makes goals more achievable, but also builds momentum and confidence. By shifting your focus from perfection to progress, you allow yourself to appreciate the journey of growth and learning, recognizing that each step forward is a success in its own right.

Building resilience against self-doubt requires patience and practice. As you integrate these strategies into your leadership style, you'll find that self-doubt becomes less of an impediment and more of a challenge that you can face with confidence and clarity.

2.4 CELEBRATING SUCCESSES AND OWNING ACHIEVEMENTS

In the fast-paced world of leadership, it can be easy to overlook personal victories in the pursuit of the next goal. Yet, acknowledging your accomplishments is important. Recognizing your achievements, both big and small, boosts confidence and reinforces your sense of self-worth. Take a moment to reflect on the milestones you've reached. Consider the projects you've led, the challenges you've overcome, and the skills you've honed. Reflecting on these successes reminds you of your capabilities and the growth you've achieved. This practice is not about dwelling on the past, but about acknowledging the journey and celebrating the progress made.

Creating a success portfolio is an effective way to document and celebrate your achievements. This portfolio serves as a tangible reminder of your capabilities and accomplishments, reinforcing your confidence during moments of doubt. You can compile this portfolio digitally or physically, using formats that best suit your needs. A digital portfolio might include presentations, reports, and emails that highlight your contributions, while a physical version could feature certificates, awards, and personal notes. This collection becomes a go-to resource for inspiration, especially when facing new challenges. It's your personal record of success, showcasing the value you bring to your role.

Sharing your success stories with peers can further reinforce your self-worth and inspire others. Platforms like LinkedIn, professional networks, or even team meetings provide opportunities to share your achievements. Discussing your experiences celebrates your accomplishments and also encourages a culture of openness and support within your professional community. Sharing can also lead to valuable feedback and connections, further enhancing your leadership growth. Remember, your success stories are not just about you; they can motivate and guide others who might face similar challenges. By sharing, you contribute to a collective pool of knowl-edge and support that benefits everyone.

To consistently acknowledge and celebrate your achievements, consider establishing personal rituals. These rituals can be simple yet meaningful, serving as regular reminders of your progress and successes. One idea is gratitude journaling, where you write down accomplishments and express gratitude for them. This practice high-lights your successes and fosters a positive mindset, focusing on what you have achieved rather than what remains undone. Another idea might be setting aside time each month to review your success portfolio, perhaps over a cup of coffee or during a quiet evening. These rituals become moments of reflection and celebration, grounding you in the recognition of your abilities.

By regularly acknowledging your achievements, you cultivate a mindset that values progress and growth. This practice counters the narrative of imposter syndrome, which often dismisses success as mere luck or external factors. In recognizing and celebrating your successes, you affirm your role as a capable and accomplished leader, ready to tackle new challenges with confidence.

2.5 CRAFTING A PERSONAL CONFIDENCE TOOLKIT

Creating a personal confidence toolkit is like assembling your own set of tools to tackle the challenges that come with leadership. This toolkit is not one-size-fits-all; it should be tailored to your unique needs and preferences. Start by gathering resources that inspire and uplift you. Books that resonate with your leadership style, podcasts that offer fresh perspectives, and quotes that speak to your soul can all find a place in this collection. Congrats, this book is already tool #1 in your toolkit! Consider podcasts like Dare to Lead by Brené Brown, with episodes that delve into the power of vulnerability and authenticity. Quotes from leaders you admire can serve as quick reminders of your strength and capability. Keep these resources easily accessible, whether on your bookshelf, in your podcast queue, or pinned to a board in your workspace. When doubt creeps in, turn to your toolkit for a boost of confidence and perspective.

Another powerful component of your confidence toolkit is a personal mantra. Similar to an affirmation, a mantra is a short, impactful phrase that you can repeat to yourself in moments of self-doubt. It acts as a mental anchor, grounding you in your capabilities and potential. To create your mantra, think about what you need to hear or see in those challenging moments. It might be something like, "I am capable and resilient," or "I trust in my ability to lead." These words should resonate deeply with you, reflecting your strengths and aspirations. Once you've crafted your mantra, print it out and hang it up on your wall. Also, practice saying it during quiet moments or when self-doubt arises. Over time, this practice reinforces your confidence, helping you approach challenges with a calm, assured mindset.

Identifying support systems is also crucial in building and maintaining confidence. Look around you at the people who uplift and encourage you. These might be mentors, colleagues, friends, or family members who believe in your potential and provide honest feedback. Engaging with a network of supportive individuals can be incredibly empowering. Seek out communities and forums where you can connect with peers who share similar experiences. Professional networking groups, women's leadership circles, or online communities can offer a sense of belonging and a platform for exchanging ideas and advice. These connections bolster your confidence, while they provide a wealth of knowledge and support as you navigate your leadership journey.

Reflecting on past successes is another technique to strengthen your confidence. When facing a new challenge, recall a time when you overcame a similar obstacle. Delve into the details of that experience —what strategies did you use, what strengths did you draw upon, and how did you feel upon achieving your goal? This process can be illuminating, revealing patterns of success and resilience that you might overlook in the moment. Techniques like creating a "success storyboard" can be helpful. This involves mapping out key victories in your career, highlighting the skills and attributes that contributed to each success. By revisiting these achievements, you remind yourself of your capabilities, building a reservoir of confidence that you can draw upon whenever needed.

Your personal confidence toolkit is a dynamic, evolving resource. As you grow and develop as a leader, continue to update it with new tools and strategies that resonate with your evolving needs. Whether it's a new book that inspires you, a fresh mantra that aligns with your current challenges, or new connections that enrich your network, let your toolkit reflect your journey.

2.6 MENTORSHIP FOR OVERCOMING IMPOSTER SYNDROME

Mentorship stands as a beacon of support for those grappling with imposter syndrome, offering guidance and reassurance when self-doubt threatens to overshadow achievements. An effective mentor can provide a fresh perspective, helping you navigate uncertainties while reinforcing your strengths. Look for someone who exhibits qualities such as empathy, patience, and a willingness to share their experiences. They should be someone who understands the challenges of leadership and appreciates the nuances of your personal journey. A mentor with a diverse background can offer a wealth of insight, having navigated similar obstacles themselves. They become a sounding board, providing feedback that is both candid and constructive, encouraging you to view setbacks as stepping stones rather than roadblocks.

Building a mentorship relationship requires intentional effort and openness. Start by identifying potential mentors within your network or industry who possess qualities you admire. When reaching out, be clear about your goals and what you hope to gain from the relationship. A well-crafted introductory message can set the tone, expressing genuine interest in learning from their experiences. Once the connection is established, nurture the relationship through regular communication and meetings. Be respectful of their time, and ensure that interactions are mutually beneficial. A mentor-mentee relationship thrives on reciprocal engagement, where both parties share and learn from each other. Consider discussing specific topics or challenges you face, inviting your mentor to offer insights and advice based on their experiences.

Within these mentorship conversations, openly exchanging experiences related to imposter syndrome can be incredibly liberating. Sharing these personal stories with someone who has likely faced similar doubts helps demystify the feelings of inadequacy. Use conversation starters that encourage this exchange, such as, "Have you ever felt out of place in your role, and how did you overcome it?" or "What strategies have you found most effective in dealing with self-doubt?" These discussions provide practical strategies and foster a deeper connection, reinforcing the idea that you are not alone in this experience. Your mentor's insights can illuminate pathways through the murkiness of self-doubt, offering tangible steps to address and overcome these challenges.

While the mentee gains from the mentor's wisdom and experience, the mentor also find value in the relationship. Mentors often report a sense of satisfaction and purpose in guiding emerging leaders, drawing inspiration from their mentees' fresh perspectives and innovative ideas. This dynamic creates a symbiotic relationship where both parties grow and evolve. Successful mentorships often become lifelong connections, where both individuals continue to support and learn from each other, even as roles and responsibilities evolve. These relationships highlight the importance of collaboration and shared growth in leadership, emphasizing that while the path to leadership may be individual, it is never walked alone.

As we navigate the complexities of leadership, mentorship becomes a vital tool in building confidence and resilience. Through these relationships, we learn to see beyond our self-imposed limitations, embracing our potential and capabilities. The journey through imposter syndrome becomes less daunting when shared with others who understand its nuances. With the support of mentors, we can challenge our doubts, celebrate our successes, and continue to grow as leaders. As we look ahead, the next chapter explores how these foundational skills can be applied to navigate the challenges of gender bias and stereotypes in leadership.

SKILL #3 - NAVIGATING GENDER BIAS AND STEREOTYPES

I still remember my first boardroom presentation vividly. As I walked in, I could feel the weight of expectations pressing down on me, a constant reminder that I had to prove myself in a male-dominated space. The meeting began, and the conversation flowed, but then I heard it—a seemingly innocuous remark about how articulate I was "for a woman." It was a stark reminder of the subtle biases that persist in workplaces everywhere. Such comments, often brushed off as compliments, represent a form of microaggression that can undermine confidence and reinforce stereotypes. While these instances might seem minor in isolation, their cumulative effect can be deeply damaging, creating barriers that hinder career growth and impact team dynamics.

3.1 THE IMPACT OF MICROAGGRESSIONS

Microaggressions are pervasive and can manifest in various forms, often going unnoticed by those not directly affected. They include comments or actions that subtly express prejudices, usually toward marginalized groups. In the workplace, these might take the form of a colleague expressing surprise at a woman's technical expertise or questioning her decisions more harshly than her male counterparts. During meetings, women might be interrupted more frequently, or their ideas might be attributed to male colleagues. These scenarios, though subtle, contribute to a culture where women feel under-valued and marginalized. The reality is that these biases aren't always intentional, but their impact is significant. They can erode self-esteem, increase stress, and lead to feelings of isolation, ulti-mately affecting job satisfaction and productivity.

Understanding the long-term effects of biases is crucial. Research indicates that microaggressions can have a profound impact on career progression, especially for women. According to the "Women in the Workplace 2023" report, microaggressions are a significant barrier to women's advancement. They affect not only individual morale, but also team dynamics, creating environments where women may feel hesitant to speak up or take on leadership roles. Over time, these biases contribute to the "broken rung" phenomenon, where women are promoted at lower rates than men, and this disparity compounds as they move up the corporate ladder. The ripple effects of microaggressions extend beyond individual careers, influencing organizational culture and perpetuating gender inequities.

Developing awareness of these subtle biases requires intentional effort. Bias recognition workshops can be instrumental in helping individuals identify and address these behaviors. These workshops provide a safe space to explore unconscious biases and learn how they manifest in daily interactions. They often include role-playing scenarios that simulate common workplace situations, allowing participants to practice recognizing and addressing microaggres-sions. Self-monitoring exercises are another effective tool. These involve reflecting on personal interactions and considering whether any biases might have influenced behavior. Keeping a journal where you note instances of bias, whether experienced or observed, can enhance self-awareness and promote personal growth. By actively engaging in these practices, you can become more attuned to subtle biases and take steps to mitigate their impact.

Creating an environment that encourages open dialogue about biases and microaggressions is essential. To foster such an atmosphere, it's important to establish clear guidelines for initiating conversations around these issues. Start by creating a culture of trust, where team members feel safe to express their concerns without fear of retaliation. Encourage open discussions by setting aside dedicated time during meetings to address diversity and inclusion topics. Use inclusive language and model respectful behavior, demonstrating a commitment to addressing biases head-on. When addressing microaggressions, approach the conversation with empathy and a willingness to listen. Remember that these discussions can be sensitive, and it's crucial to approach them with care and consideration, aiming to educate rather than alienate.

Reflective Exercise: Identifying and Addressing Microaggressions

- Reflect on a recent workplace interaction. Did you notice any subtle biases or microaggressions?
- How did these interactions make you feel, and what impact did they have on your sense of belonging and confidence?
- Consider how you might address similar situations in the future. What language or strategies could you use to open a dialogue about the bias?
- Share your reflections with a trusted colleague or mentor, inviting their perspective and advice on navigating these challenges.

By fostering awareness and encouraging open dialogue, you can contribute to a workplace culture that values diversity and inclusion, paving the way for more equitable opportunities and empowering all team members to thrive.

3.2 STRATEGIES FOR ADDRESSING GENDER BIAS IN MEETINGS

Meetings are a microcosm of workplace culture, often reflecting broader societal dynamics, including gender biases. In these settings, the subtle yet pervasive influence of gender dynamics can shape interactions and outcomes. Studies have shown that women are more frequently interrupted or spoken over in meetings, while their contributions may go unrecognized or attributed to others. This pattern undermines confidence and diminishes the value of diverse perspectives. Recognizing these dynamics is the first step toward change. By observing who speaks, who is interrupted, and who receives credit, you can begin to uncover the invisible patterns that affect meeting dynamics. It's crucial to remain vigilant and aware, as these biases often operate beneath the surface, affecting team morale and productivity.

Implementing meeting protocols can help ensure that all voices are heard and valued. One effective strategy is to establish a "no interruption" policy, where participants agree to let each speaker finish their thoughts before responding. This simple rule fosters an atmosphere of respect and ensures that everyone has the opportunity to contribute without fear of being cut off. Additionally, consider rotating roles for meeting facilitation. Assigning different team members to lead discussions or take notes distributes responsibility and empowers individuals to engage more fully. This approach encourages diverse participation and ensures that credit is distributed fairly. By formalizing these practices, meetings can become more inclusive and productive, reflecting a culture of equity and respect.

Empowering women to speak up in meetings requires both individual and organizational commitment. As a woman in leadership, it's vital to assert your presence confidently. Techniques for effective communication can boost this effort. Start by preparing thoroughly for meetings, knowing your material, and anticipating questions. This preparation builds confidence and allows you to speak with authority. Use assertive body language, such as maintaining eye contact and using a strong, clear voice. These non-verbal cues signal confidence and command attention. Practice speaking up early in meetings, as this sets a precedent for active participation. Encouragingly, many organizations are beginning to recognize the importance of amplifying women's voices, providing platforms and opportunities for women to lead discussions and present ideas.

Educating colleagues about inclusive practices is a vital component of addressing gender bias in meetings. Providing resources and training can raise awareness and foster a culture of inclusivity. Workshops on inclusive meeting practices can be particularly effective. These sessions can explore topics such as the impact of unconscious biases, strategies for equitable participation, and the importance of acknowledging contributions. Participants can engage in role-playing exercises to practice inclusive behaviors, gaining insights into their own biases and learning how to support others. Educational materials on gender bias, such as articles, videos, and case studies, can supplement these workshops, offering additional perspectives and resources for continued learning. By equipping all team members with the knowledge and tools to recognize and address biases, organizations can create environments where everyone feels valued and empowered.

Interactive Element: Meeting Protocol Checklist

- Establish a "no interruption" policy to ensure all voices are heard.

- Rotate meeting facilitation roles to promote diverse participation.
- Encourage assertive communication techniques for all participants.
- Provide workshops and resources on inclusive meeting practices.

Incorporating these strategies into regular meeting routines can transform interactions, allowing for an environment where individuals feel respected and valued. By addressing gender biases head-on, you set the stage for more equitable and productive collaboration, paving the way for innovation and success.

3.3 BUILDING ALLIES AND ADVOCATES FOR GENDER EQUALITY

Identifying potential allies within your workplace is a critical step in promoting gender equality. Allies are those colleagues who understand the challenges women face and are willing to support and advocate for change. They are not just sympathetic listeners, but active participants in fostering an inclusive environment. Effective allies possess certain characteristics that make them stand out. They are empathetic, open-minded, and committed to social justice. They ask questions, listen actively, and learn from the experiences of others. These allies are not afraid to speak up against biases or inequalities, even when it is uncomfortable. Their advocacy is not just performative; it is rooted in a genuine desire to create a fair and equitable workplace. Identifying these individuals can sometimes involve observing who consistently supports diversity initiatives or who speaks out against unfair practices.

Once potential allies are identified, the next step is to cultivate allyship through strategic and meaningful relationships. Building supportive relationships involves more than just identifying allies; it requires creating opportunities for collaboration and mutual support. Joint advocacy projects can serve as a powerful platform for this collaboration. These projects might involve organizing workshops on gender equality, launching campaigns to promote diversity, or developing mentorship programs for women. These initiatives promote gender equality and strengthen the bond between allies, fostering a sense of shared purpose. Additionally, participating in allyship training sessions can further solidify these relationships. These sessions provide a structured environment for learning and dialogue, equipping allies with the skills to advocate effectively. They can cover topics such as recognizing unconscious biases, effective allyship practices, and strategies for supporting marginalized colleagues. Training sessions also offer a safe space to address questions or concerns, facilitating open and honest discussions that drive real change.

Leveraging ally networks is another essential strategy for advancing gender equality. These networks comprise individuals and groups committed to promoting diversity and inclusion within the workplace. They can be formal, such as employee resource groups, or informal, like social circles that connect over shared values. Successful ally networks often involve collaboration across departments and levels of an organization, creating a broad base of support. Within these networks, members share resources, best practices, and experiences, amplifying their collective impact. An example of a successful ally network might be a company-wide initiative that pairs senior leaders with emerging female talent for mentorship and advocacy. By tapping into these networks, you can access a wealth of knowledge and support, strengthening your efforts to promote gender equality. Furthermore, these networks can serve as a platform for raising awareness, sharing success stories, and rallying support for gender equality initiatives.

Encouraging male allies to actively participate in gender equality advocacy is crucial. Men hold a significant share of leadership positions and can leverage their influence to drive meaningful change. Engaging men as allies involves inviting them into the conversation and highlighting the benefits of gender equality for everyone. Initiatives to engage male allies might include workshops that focus on understanding gender dynamics, highlighting the role of men in fostering inclusion, and providing tools for effective allyship. Stories of male allies making a difference can also be powerful motivators. Sharing examples of men who have successfully advocated for gender equality demonstrates the positive impact they can have. These stories can inspire others to take action, illustrating how allyship can lead to tangible improvements in workplace culture. By working together, male and female allies can create a more inclusive environment that benefits all employees.

Building allies and advocates for gender equality is not a one-time effort; it requires ongoing commitment and collaboration. Allies must remain vigilant, challenging biases and supporting initiatives that promote diversity and inclusion. Through these efforts, you can contribute to creating a workplace where everyone has the opportunity to thrive, regardless of gender.

3.4 TRANSFORMING BIAS INTO OPPORTUNITIES FOR GROWTH

Bias in the workplace often feels like an insurmountable obstacle, but it can also be a catalyst for growth and transformation. It's about shifting perception, viewing these biases not just as hindrances, but as opportunities to learn and evolve. Each encounter with bias can serve as a mirror, reflecting areas of personal growth and resilience. When faced with a biased comment or action, instead of internalizing it, consider asking yourself, "What can this teach me?" Reframing these negative experiences into learning moments allows you to extract valuable insights. This approach enhances personal development and also inspires organizational change. By analyzing these situations, you gain a deeper understanding of the systemic issues at play and can develop strategies to address them. Embracing this mindset transforms bias from a barrier into a stepping stone toward personal empowerment and organizational progress.

To effectively disrupt biases, it's crucial to employ strategies that change the narrative. The "calling in" versus "calling out" approach offers a nuanced way to address bias. Calling out involves directly confronting a bias, which can sometimes lead to defensiveness or conflict. In contrast, calling in focuses on engaging the individual in a private, empathetic conversation aimed at understanding and education. This method fosters a more constructive dialogue, encouraging reflection and change without alienating the person involved. Consider a scenario where a colleague makes an uninformed comment. Instead of publicly reprimanding them, you might invite them for a one-on-one discussion to explore the impact of their words. This approach promotes a culture of learning and accountability, transforming potentially divisive situations into opportunities for growth and understanding. By adopting these techniques, you contribute to a more inclusive and supportive work environment.

Bias incidents also provide teachable moments that can educate and inform others. Sharing personal experiences with bias, whether through storytelling or formal presentations, can help raise awareness and foster empathy. Creating educational content from these experiences, such as workshops or articles, allows you to reach a wider audience. These platforms can be powerful tools for illustrating the real-world impact of bias and offering actionable solutions. For example, you might develop a training module that includes case studies of bias incidents and strategies for addressing them. By doing so, you educate your peers and empower them to become advocates for change. These shared experiences can cultivate a collective understanding of the challenges faced by marginalized groups, encouraging a proactive approach to fostering equity and inclusion.

3.5 LEVERAGING EMOTIONAL INTELLIGENCE TO OVERCOME STEREOTYPES

Navigating the intricacies of workplace dynamics often requires more than just technical skills and knowledge. Emotional intelligence (EI) plays a crucial role in how we perceive, manage, and influence our own emotions and those of others. In the context of stereotypes, EI becomes a powerful tool. It allows us to understand and counteract the biases that can cloud judgment and decision-making. At its core, emotional intelligence encompasses self-awareness, self-regulation, motivation, empathy, and social skills. These components work together to enhance our ability to navigate complex social environments with grace and effectiveness. Self-awareness helps us recognize our emotional triggers and biases, while self-regulation allows us to manage these emotions constructively. Motivation drives us to pursue goals despite setbacks, and empathy enables us to understand others' perspectives, which is crucial in dismantling stereotypes. Social skills facilitate effective communication and relationship building, essential in fostering an inclusive workplace.

Empathy, a key component of emotional intelligence, is particularly vital in challenging stereotypes. It involves putting oneself in another's shoes, understanding their experiences and feelings. This understanding is the first step in breaking down preconceived notions and biases. Empathy-building exercises can aid in developing this skill. These might include active listening activities, where you focus on truly hearing and understanding a colleague's perspective without judgment or interruption. Another exercise could involve reflecting on your own experiences of being misunderstood or stereotyped and considering how those experiences shape your interactions with others. By cultivating empathy, you open the door to more meaningful connections and a deeper appreciation of diversity. This shift in perspective helps challenge existing stereotypes and fosters a more inclusive environment where everyone feels valued and understood.

Practicing self-regulation in situations where bias is present is another critical aspect of leveraging emotional intelligence. As mentioned before, self-regulation involves maintaining composure and responding thoughtfully rather than reacting impulsively. In high-pressure scenarios where stereotypes may arise, it becomes essential to keep a cool head. Techniques for calming responses in stressful situations can help center your thoughts and reduce anxiety. When you find yourself in a situation where a stereotype is being perpetuated, take a moment to breathe deeply and assess the situation before responding. This pause allows you to choose your words and actions carefully, helping to defuse tension and promote constructive dialogue. Additionally, developing a habit of reflecting on these interactions afterward can provide valuable insights into how you can improve your response in the future. By practicing self-regulation, you manage your own emotions effectively and set an example for others, promoting a culture of thoughtful and respectful communication.

Fostering inclusive perspectives through emotional intelligence involves creating an environment where diverse viewpoints are not only welcomed, but celebrated. This requires a deliberate effort to cultivate an inclusive mindset, one that values differences and seeks to understand them. Scenario-based training can be an effective way to develop this mindset. These trainings present real-life situations where participants must navigate complex interpersonal dynamics, encouraging them to apply emotional intelligence skills to resolve challenges. For example, a scenario might involve mediating a disagreement between team members with differing cultural perspectives. By practicing these scenarios, individuals learn to approach differences with curiosity rather than judgment, opening the door to richer, more collaborative interactions. This training not only enhances the individual's ability to navigate diverse environments, but also contributes to a broader culture of inclusivity within the organization. By leveraging emotional intelligence in this way, you help create a workplace where everyone feels a sense of belonging and empowerment, paving the way for greater collaboration and innovation.

3.6 CREATING INCLUSIVE WORK ENVIRONMENTS

To truly foster inclusivity within your workplace, it's essential to first assess the current level of inclusion. An inclusivity audit offers a structured way to evaluate how welcoming and equitable your environment is. This process involves examining various aspects of the workplace, such as hiring practices, team dynamics, and overall culture. Start by gathering feedback from employees through anonymous surveys that ask about their experiences and perceptions. Include questions about whether they feel respected, valued, and comfortable expressing their identities. Analyze the diversity of your workforce at all levels, particularly in leadership roles, to identify any gaps or disparities. Review company policies to see if they're inclusive and equitable. By understanding where your organization stands, you can identify areas for improvement and develop targeted strategies to enhance inclusivity. This proactive approach not only helps create a more welcoming environment but also boosts employee morale and retention.

Once you have a clear understanding of your workplace's inclusivity, the next step is to implement policies and practices that promote equality and diversity. One effective strategy is to introduce flexible work arrangements, which can accommodate a diverse range of needs, from parental responsibilities to personal health considerations. Flexibility in the workplace shows a commitment to supporting employees as individuals, not just workers. Additionally, consider developing mentorship programs that pair employees from underrepresented groups with experienced mentors who can offer guidance and support. Establish clear anti-discrimination policies and ensure they are not only written, but actively enforced. Encourage diverse hiring panels to reduce unconscious bias in recruitment, and set diversity targets to hold the organization accountable. These policies signal to employees that the company values diversity and is committed to creating an equitable workplace.

Promoting continuous education and training on diversity and inclusion is crucial to maintaining a culture of inclusivity. Regular diversity training programs can educate employees on the importance of inclusivity, equipping them with the knowledge to recognize and address biases. These programs can cover topics such as unconscious bias, cultural competence, and inclusive communication. Encourage all employees, from entry-level staff to executives, to participate in these trainings, demonstrating that inclusivity is a collective responsibility. Additionally, provide resources such as books, articles, and online courses for employees to explore on their own. Consider inviting guest speakers or hosting panel discussions to share diverse perspectives and experiences. By prioritizing continuous learning, you foster an environment where employees feel empowered to contribute to an inclusive culture.

Celebrating successes in diversity and inclusion is an important way to acknowledge progress and motivate continued efforts. Annual diversity and inclusion retrospectives can provide an opportunity to reflect on achievements and set goals for the future. During these retrospectives, highlight stories of individuals or teams who have made significant contributions to creating an inclusive workplace. Recognition programs can also be implemented to honor leaders who exemplify inclusive practices. These programs celebrate achievements and set benchmarks for others to aspire to. Publicly acknowledging and rewarding inclusive behavior reinforces its importance and encourages others to follow suit.

Creating an inclusive work environment is a continuous effort that requires commitment from everyone. By assessing inclusivity, implementing equitable policies, promoting ongoing education, and celebrating diversity, you pave the way for a workplace where everyone feels valued and empowered.

SKILL #4 - BUILDING A SUPPORTIVE NETWORK

Picture this: the bustling energy of a conference room, filled with professionals from diverse backgrounds, each with their own stories and expertise. Through the chatter and exchange of business cards, you find yourself engaged in a conversation that sparks a new idea. This moment is not just an instance of social interaction; it's a gateway to opportunities that can shape your career. Building a supportive network is more than just making connections—it's about creating a web of relationships that provide guidance, inspiration, and opportunities for growth. Networking with purpose and intention ensures that each interaction contributes meaningfully to your professional journey.

4.1 THE ART OF PURPOSEFUL NETWORKING

Purposeful networking involves approaching connections with clear goals and objectives. It's about knowing what you want to achieve and seeking out interactions that align with these aspirations. Begin by setting specific networking goals. Consider what you hope to accomplish through your network, whether it's gaining industry insights, finding a mentor, or exploring new career opportunities. Having well-defined goals ensures that your networking efforts are targeted and productive. Once you've established these goals, identify key industry events that align with them. Conferences, seminars, and workshops are excellent venues to meet individuals who share your professional interests.

Crafting an effective elevator pitch is a crucial strategy in building meaningful connections. An elevator pitch is a brief, persuasive speech that introduces you and your professional background. It should be concise yet compelling, capturing the essence of who you are and what you do. Practice crafting and refining your pitch to ensure it resonates with diverse audiences. Consider including key achievements or unique skills that set you apart. The goal is to spark interest and leave a memorable impression. Additionally, focus on techniques for maintaining long-term relationships. Networking isn't just about the initial contact; it's about nurturing connections over time. Follow up with new contacts, express genuine interest in their work, and find ways to offer value. Building relationships requires effort and consistency, but the rewards are substantial.

Recognizing diverse opportunities for networking is essential in expanding your professional circle. Beyond traditional industry events, look for opportunities in volunteering for professional organizations. These roles allow you to contribute to a cause and also provide access to a network of like-minded individuals. Volunteering can open doors to new connections and experiences, enriching your professional journey. Think outside the box and explore unconventional settings, such as community groups or interest-based meetups, where you can connect with professionals from different fields. Each interaction, no matter how informal, holds the potential for collaboration and learning. Embrace the diversity of opportunities available, and approach each with curiosity and openness.

Evaluating and refining your networking strategies is a continuous process. Regularly assess the effectiveness of your networking efforts to ensure they align with your evolving goals. Networking feedback loops can be a valuable tool in this process. Seek feedback from trusted peers or mentors on your networking approach, and be open to suggestions for improvement. This feedback provides insights into how others perceive your interactions and can guide adjustments. Conduct a personal networking SWOT analysis to identify your strengths, weaknesses, opportunities, and threats in networking. This exercise can reveal areas for growth and help you leverage your strengths more effectively.

Interactive Element: Personal Networking SWOT Analysis

- **Strengths**: What are your networking strengths? Consider your communication skills, industry knowledge, or ability to connect with diverse individuals.
- **Weaknesses**: Identify areas that need improvement. Are there skills or situations where you feel less confident?
- **Opportunities**: What opportunities exist for expanding your network? Think about upcoming events, potential mentors, or professional groups.
- **Threats**: What challenges might you face in networking? Consider time constraints, competition, or biases you may encounter.

Reflect on these points and use them to develop a plan for enhancing your networking approach. By doing so, you strengthen your network and position yourself for greater career success. Networking is not static; it's dynamic and requires adaptability. By continually evaluating and refining your strategies, you ensure that your network remains robust and relevant.

4.2 FINDING AND NURTURING MENTORSHIP RELATIONSHIPS

Mentorship is a cornerstone of career development, offering insights and guidance that can accelerate personal and professional growth. We previously talked about mentorship specific to overcoming imposter syndrome, but let's talk about mentorship as a part of your ongoing support system. Having a mentor, particularly in leadership roles, provides a unique opportunity to learn from someone who has navigated similar paths. They can help you build confidence, broaden your perspective, and develop the skills necessary to excel. The benefits are numerous: mentors can open doors to new opportunities, offer constructive feedback, and provide the encouragement needed to push beyond perceived limits. In a world where women often face unique hurdles, mentorship becomes even more critical, offering a supportive environment to grow and thrive.

Identifying potential mentors requires thoughtful consideration. A good mentor should align with your personal and professional goals, sharing values and ambitions that resonate with your own. Look for individuals whose career paths and professional styles you admire. These are often people who have achieved success in areas that you aspire to explore. Characteristics of a good mentor include a willingness to share their experiences, the ability to listen and provide meaningful feedback, and a genuine interest in your development. Networking events are fertile grounds for meeting potential mentors, with seasoned professionals who might be willing to take on a mentoring role. Pay attention to speakers and panelists who inspire you, and don't hesitate to reach out and express your interest in learning from them.

Once you've established a mentorship relationship, nurturing it is key to ensure it remains productive and beneficial for both parties. Regular check-ins and goal-setting meetings help maintain momentum and focus. These interactions provide an opportunity to discuss progress, challenges, and new goals. It's important to approach these meetings with clear objectives and a willingness to receive feedback. Reciprocity is also crucial in mentorship. While the mentor provides guidance and support, the mentee should bring their own insights and enthusiasm to the table. This mutual exchange enriches the relationship, fostering a dynamic where both parties feel valued and engaged.

Leveraging mentorship for career advancement involves actively seeking insights and opportunities through the relationship. Successful mentor-mentee partnerships often demonstrate how mentorship can lead to tangible career benefits. Consider the case of a young executive who, through her mentor's guidance, gained access to leadership training programs and networking opportunities that were pivotal in her career progression. These partnerships highlight the importance of being proactive in seeking advice and exploring new avenues suggested by your mentor. Use the insights gained from your mentor to navigate complex decisions and capitalize on new opportunities. A mentor can also introduce you to influential contacts or recommend you for roles that align with your aspirations. This network expansion can be a game-changer, providing access to circles that might otherwise be out of reach.

In the realm of mentorship, the relationship should be dynamic and adaptable, evolving as you grow and encounter new challenges. As you progress, your goals may shift, and your mentorship needs may change. Open communication is essential in navigating these transitions, ensuring that both you and your mentor are on the same page. This adaptability allows the relationship to remain relevant and supportive, reflecting your ongoing development. Through mentorship, you gain not only a guide, but also a partner in your leadership journey, someone who believes in your potential and helps illuminate the path ahead.

4.3 CREATING A PERSONAL BOARD OF ADVISORS

Imagine having a group of seasoned professionals, each bringing their unique perspective to the table, ready to offer insight and guidance whenever you need it. This is the concept of a personal board of advisors. Unlike a traditional company board, this board is composed of individuals who are solely focused on your growth and development. Each member plays a specific role, contributing their expertise and experience to help you navigate challenges and seize opportunities. These advisors can be mentors, industry experts, peers, or even friends, each offering a different lens through which to view your career.

Selecting advisors with diverse expertise is crucial. Look for individuals who bring varied backgrounds and experiences and who know you from all areas of your life, ensuring a well-rounded board. For instance, you might include someone with financial acumen, another with deep industry knowledge, another who excels in leadership, and a companion who sees you thriving as a mother. This diversity broadens your perspective and provides access to a wealth of knowledge and networks. When choosing advisors, consider their willingness to invest time in your development and their ability to offer honest, constructive feedback. Their alignment with your values and goals is equally important, as this ensures that their guidance is relevant and actionable.

Establishing clear objectives for your advisory board is essential to maximizing its effectiveness. Define what you hope to achieve with the board's support. Are you looking to advance in your career, pivot to a new industry, or develop specific skills? Clearly articulating these goals helps focus the board's efforts and provides a framework for your interactions. Regular strategic planning sessions with your advisors can facilitate this process, offering a platform to discuss progress, refine goals, and address any challenges. During these sessions, encourage open dialogue and welcome diverse viewpoints, as this can lead to innovative solutions and strategies that you might not have considered.

Engagement with your advisors should be consistent and ongoing. Regular interaction ensures that the relationship remains dynamic and productive. Consider scheduling quarterly meetings to discuss updates, seek advice, and explore new opportunities. These meetings provide a structured environment for meaningful discussions and decision-making. In between these formal sessions, maintain open lines of communication through emails, calls, or messaging. This ongoing dialogue strengthens your relationship and allows you to tap into their expertise whenever needed.

The personal board of advisors is not just a sounding board; it is a strategic asset that can significantly impact your development. By leveraging the combined wisdom and experience of your advisors, you gain a competitive edge, one that is informed by diverse perspectives and insights. As you engage with this board, remember that the relationship is reciprocal. While you benefit from their guidance, they too gain from your fresh perspectives and enthusiasm. This mutual exchange enriches the advisory experience, fostering a partnership that is both rewarding and empowering.

4.4 NAVIGATING NETWORKING IN MALE-DOMINATED SPACES

In male-dominated industries, navigating professional networks can feel like treading through uncharted waters. Women often face unique challenges in these environments. The barriers are not always overt; sometimes, they manifest in subtle ways that can undermine confidence and hinder progress. Common networking obstacles include being overlooked or underestimated and having to work harder to prove credibility. These settings may also present fewer opportunities for women to engage in informal networking activities, such as post-meeting social gatherings, where many connections are made. The lack of representation can lead to feelings of isolation, making it harder to build the supportive networks that are crucial for career advancement.

Despite these challenges, effective networking strategies can significantly enhance your ability to build meaningful connections. Assertive communication is key. It involves expressing your ideas and intentions clearly and confidently, without aggression. This can be achieved by maintaining eye contact, using a firm voice, and ensuring that your contributions during discussions are both heard and acknowledged. Additionally, finding common ground can help in building rapport. Shared interests, whether professional or personal, can serve as a bridge, making interactions more comfortable and genuine. By engaging in conversations that highlight these commonalities, you create a foundation of mutual respect and understanding, making it easier to foster lasting professional relationships.

In male-dominated fields, your allies can play a crucial role in advocating for inclusivity and opening doors to new opportunities. Successful allyship is evident in various industries. For example, male leaders who mentor and sponsor female colleagues contribute significantly to their career advancement. These allies can provide guidance, offer introductions to key contacts, and help amplify your voice in important conversations. Building these alliances requires identifying individuals who share your commitment to inclusion and are willing to actively support your professional growth.

Turning networking challenges into opportunities for growth involves reframing obstacles as learning experiences. Consider the stories of women who have thrived in male-dominated spaces by leveraging their unique perspectives and skills. In the automotive industry, for instance, female engineers have driven innovation by bringing diverse viewpoints to traditionally homogenous teams. These women have used the challenges they faced to fuel their determination and creativity, ultimately carving out influential roles for themselves. By viewing setbacks as opportunities to learn and adapt, you can build resilience and develop strategies that address immediate challenges and pave the way for long-term success.

4.5 LEVERAGING DIGITAL PLATFORMS FOR NETWORKING

In today's digital age, networking has transcended physical boundaries, opening up a world of opportunities through online platforms. The benefits of digital networking are immense, providing access to professionals around the globe from the comfort of your home. Platforms like LinkedIn and Twitter serve as virtual meeting places where you can connect with industry leaders, peers, and potential collaborators. LinkedIn, with over a billion users, is particularly renowned for its professional focus, offering features that allow you to showcase your skills, share achievements, and discover opportunities that align with your career goals. Twitter, while less formal, offers a dynamic environment for engaging in industry conversations and staying abreast of the latest trends and developments. Meanwhile, professional forums cater to niche interests, fostering communities where you can dive deep into specific topics and build connections with like-minded individuals.

Building a strong online presence is essential for maximizing the potential of these platforms. Start by optimizing your LinkedIn profile to ensure it reflects your professional brand. Use a professional photo, craft a compelling headline, and write a summary that highlights your skills and accomplishments. This is your digital first impression, so make it count. Regularly update your profile with new achievements, skills, and experiences to keep it current. Engaging with industry-specific content further enhances your online presence. Share articles, comment on posts, and participate in discussions relevant to your field. This demonstrates your expertise and also increases your visibility among peers and potential connections.

Active participation in online communities is another key aspect of leveraging digital platforms effectively. By contributing to discussions in professional groups, you can establish yourself as a thought leader and gain insights from others. Whether it's a LinkedIn group focused on your industry or a forum dedicated to a specific skill, these spaces offer valuable opportunities to learn and connect. Hosting virtual meetups or webinars is another way to engage meaningfully with your network. These events can position you as a knowledgeable resource, attract new connections, and foster deeper relationships with existing contacts. Consider organizing sessions on topics you're passionate about or areas where you have significant expertise. This proactive approach builds your credibility and strengthens the bonds within your network.

Utilizing digital tools designed for networking efficiency can further enhance your efforts. Networking apps and Customer Relationship Management (CRM) systems streamline the process of managing your connections, ensuring no opportunity is missed. Apps like Meetup and Eventbrite help you discover and organize professional events, while platforms like LinkedIn offer built-in tools for tracking interactions and following up with contacts. CRM systems allow you to organize your contacts, set reminders for follow-ups, and track the progress of your networking goals. By integrating these tools into your routine, you can manage your network more effectively, keeping relationships active and productive.

Incorporating these digital strategies into your networking approach provides a comprehensive framework for building a robust professional network. By combining a strong online presence with active engagement and the right tools, you can create a network that supports your career ambitions and enriches your professional life with diverse perspectives and opportunities. These strategies empower you to connect with others authentically and purposefully, paving the way for meaningful collaborations and growth.

4.6 BUILDING A COMMUNITY OF SUPPORT AMONG FEMALE LEADERS

In the landscape of leadership, female support networks hold immense value. These networks are not just about professional advancement; they are about creating spaces where women can share experiences, challenges, and triumphs. Being part of a female-led community provides a sense of belonging and empowerment. These communities foster an environment where women feel safe to express themselves, exchange ideas, and support one another in their pursuits. The benefits are multifaceted: they offer mentorship, facilitate career opportunities, and provide a platform for collective advocacy. In a world where women often face unique challenges, having a network of peers who understand and empathize can be transformative. It's within these circles that women can build confidence and find the encouragement needed to push boundaries.

To build a supportive community, intentional strategies are required. Regular meetups or workshops serve as a foundation for fostering connections. Whether virtual or in-person, these gatherings create opportunities for women to engage in meaningful discussions, learn from each other, and forge lasting relationships. Hosting themed workshops on topics like leadership skills, work-life balance, or industry trends can provide valuable learning experiences and encourage participation. Additionally, creating online forums for discussion and support extends the reach of these networks. Platforms like Slack or private Facebook groups can serve as hubs where members share resources, ask questions, and offer support. These forums maintain the network's vibrancy between meetups, ensuring continuous interaction and engagement.

Encouraging collaboration and knowledge sharing within these communities enhances their effectiveness. Knowledge exchange sessions further a culture of openness. By organizing panels or discussions led by members, communities can tap into the diverse expertise within the group. These exchanges inspire innovation, foster creativity, and strengthen the collective knowledge base. The culture of collaboration nurtures an environment where members feel valued and motivated to contribute, reinforcing the network's purpose and impact.

Celebrating successes within the community reinforces the bonds among members and highlights the network's achievements. Annual awards or recognition events offer a formal occasion to acknowledge outstanding contributions and milestones. These celebrations honor individual accomplishments and inspire others by showcasing what is possible. Recognition can take various forms, from formal awards to simple shout-outs in newsletters. Sharing success stories in newsletters keeps the community informed and motivated, reminding members of the shared goals and achievements. These narratives highlight the various paths to success and demonstrate the power of a supportive network in overcoming obstacles. By celebrating together, the community fosters a sense of pride and unity, encouraging members to continue striving for excellence.

As this chapter draws to a close, the importance of building and nurturing a community of support among female leaders becomes clear. These networks are vital for personal and professional growth, offering a safe space for collaboration, learning, and celebration. By fostering such communities, we create a ripple effect that extends beyond individual members, influencing broader organizational cultures and driving systemic change. With the foundation of a strong network, female leaders are better equipped to face challenges, seize opportunities, and lead with impact.

ADD YOUR THOUGHTS TO THE CONVERSATION ON GREAT LEADERSHIP

When you take on a leadership role, the sudden realization that you have to demonstrate a host of new skills you never needed before may seem daunting. You were promoted because you are good at what you do. You are a thought leader, with knowledge to share and a work ethic that marks you among the best. Yet in your previous role, you may not have been required to utilize as many people skills —and as a manager, the way you run your team directly impacts their motivation, productivity, and commitment to your organization in the long term.

Being a manager pushes you to be your best, most comprehensive, and flexible self. It requires you to be the spark that creates diverse, forward-thinking, positive teams that embrace change instead of shying away from it. Yet it is possible to rise to all these challenges, so long as you have the information, commitment, and willingness to experiment, practice, and adapt as needed.

My aim throughout this book has been to show readers that excelling at leadership, especially as a woman, is not a mystery; it involves embracing specific strategies and techniques that can help you be your own best teacher. If these tips have put you on course to be the kind of leader you always admired, then I hope you can let others know what they will find here.

By leaving a short review on Amazon, you can let other female managers know that every day is a new opportunity to discover and utilize the skills they need to help their teams achieve even the most ambitious goals.

Thank you for your support. Thought leaders enjoy sharing the knowledge they gain. I hope you sign up for this cause and lead other readers to the information they are seeking.

Scan the QR code to leave a review.

https://www.amazon.com/review/create-review/?asin=B0F1G476KF

SKILL #5 - MAINTAINING PSYCHOLOGICAL SAFETY AND TEAM DYNAMICS

I magine stepping into a meeting where the air is thick with anticipation, yet each team member feels at ease to voice their thoughts, knowing they won't face ridicule or backlash. This is the essence of psychological safety—a concept that serves as the backbone of high-performing teams. In today's dynamic work environment, psychological safety is more than a buzzword; it is a critical element that allows teams to innovate, collaborate, and thrive. It's defined as a shared belief that the team is safe for interpersonal risk-taking. When employees feel psychologically safe, they are more likely to engage, contribute ideas, and take necessary risks without fear of negative consequences.

5.1 IDENTIFYING GAPS IN PSYCHOLOGICAL SAFETY

Assessing the current climate of your team is the first step in fostering psychological safety. To evaluate this, consider using surveys and feedback mechanisms that focus on several key indicators. Are team members hesitant to speak up during meetings? Do they feel supported when mistakes happen? These questions can help gauge the level of psychological safety present. Anonymous surveys can be particularly effective, as they allow employees to express their thoughts candidly without fear of reprisal. Regular feedback sessions, where team members are encouraged to share their experiences and perceptions openly, can also provide valuable insights into the team's dynamics. By identifying areas where psychological safety is lacking, leaders can take targeted actions to create a more supportive environment. Monitoring and sustaining psychological safety is an ongoing process that requires regular attention and commitment.

Reflection Exercise: Assessing Team Psychological Safety

- Reflect on recent team interactions. Did team members feel comfortable sharing ideas and concerns?
- Consider the feedback you've received from team members. What does it reveal about the current level of psychological safety?
- Identify any patterns or themes in the feedback. What actions can you take to address areas of concern?
- Share your reflections with a trusted colleague or mentor, seeking their perspective on fostering psychological safety within your team.

Psychological safety is not a one-time initiative but a continuous journey of growth and learning. By prioritizing this aspect of team dynamics, leaders can create an environment where every team member feels empowered to contribute, innovate, and succeed.

5.2 FACILITATING OPEN AND HONEST COMMUNICATION

In the realm of effective team dynamics, communication stands as a pillar that supports trust and collaboration. Promoting transparency in communication is vital to building this trust. When team members feel informed about goals, challenges, and changes, they are more likely to be engaged and productive. Implementing open-door policies can encourage this transparency. By being accessible and approachable, you signal to your team that their input is valued and that they can share concerns without fear of negative repercussions. Regular team updates and debriefs are also crucial. These meetings ensure everyone is on the same page, allowing you to address issues promptly and collectively. Sharing progress and setbacks openly fosters a culture where honesty and accountability are the norms, not the exceptions.

A diverse range of viewpoints enriches team discussions by offering unique insights and solutions. Encouraging these perspectives takes deliberate effort. Structured brainstorming sessions can be an effective way to gather diverse input. By setting specific guidelines for these sessions, you can ensure that all ideas are heard and considered. Round-robin discussions, where each team member is given the floor to share their thoughts, can further ensure that quieter voices are not overshadowed by more dominant ones. This approach democratizes participation and highlights the value placed on each individual's contribution, reinforcing a sense of belonging and importance within the team. As team members become accustomed to sharing their perspectives, they cultivate a more holistic approach to problem-solving, drawing from a well of varied experiences and ideas.

Communication barriers can impede the flow of ideas and information, leading to misunderstandings and reduced effectiveness. Identifying these barriers is the first step toward overcoming them. Techniques like "clear the air" meetings can help address misunderstandings before they escalate. These meetings provide a space for team members to voice grievances and clarify intentions, fostering mutual understanding and respect. Training on non-verbal communication cues is another valuable tool. Much of communication is non-verbal, and being attuned to these cues can enhance interpersonal interactions. Workshops on body language, tone, and facial expressions can equip team members with the skills to interpret and convey messages effectively. By breaking down these barriers, you create an environment where communication is fluid and efficient, enhancing overall team performance.

As reviewed briefly in Chapter 1, active listening is a critical component of effective communication, yet it is often overlooked. Developing active listening skills enables you to truly understand and value team input, leading to more informed decisions. Role-playing exercises can be a practical method to hone these skills. By simulating real-life scenarios, team members can practice listening attentively and responding appropriately. These exercises highlight the importance of empathy and patience in communication, encouraging participants to consider perspectives beyond their own. Workshops on active listening techniques further reinforce these skills, providing practical tips and strategies for everyday interactions. As active listening becomes ingrained in the team's culture, it strengthens relationships and trust, creating a more cohesive and collaborative work environment. This emphasis on listening improves communication and empowers team members to speak up, knowing their voices will be heard and respected.

In the fast-paced world of leadership, facilitating open and honest communication requires consistent effort and dedication. By nurturing transparency, encouraging diverse viewpoints, and addressing barriers, you lay the groundwork for a team dynamic that thrives on trust and collaboration. As you cultivate these communication practices, you empower your team to reach new heights of creativity and innovation, driving success for both individuals and the organization as a whole.

5.3 ENCOURAGING RISK-TAKING AND CREATIVITY

In the ever-evolving landscape of leadership, promoting a culture of experimentation stands out as a vital strategy for driving innovation and maintaining a competitive edge. Encouraging your team to take calculated risks and explore new ideas can lead to breakthroughs that propel the organization forward. Imagine a workplace where team members feel empowered to propose bold ideas, even if they might fail. This environment doesn't happen by chance; it requires intention and support. One effective way to cultivate this culture is through innovation challenges or hackathons. These events create a space where creativity is not just encouraged but expected, and where the usual constraints of daily work can be lifted temporarily. By setting aside dedicated time for these activities, you signal to your team that innovation is a priority and that their ideas are valued.

Recognizing and rewarding creative efforts is an essential component of nurturing this innovative spirit. Implementing incentive programs that celebrate innovative ideas can motivate team members to push boundaries. These programs might include financial rewards, public recognition, or opportunities for professional development. Recognition events, where creative problem-solving is highlighted and celebrated, further reinforce the value placed on innovation. During these events, showcasing successful projects and the people behind them can inspire others to think creatively and take risks. By making creativity a celebrated aspect of the workplace culture, you encourage individual contributions and foster a collective sense of ownership and pride in the team's achievements.

To support a culture of experimentation, it's crucial to provide the necessary resources for innovation. This means ensuring that teams have access to the tools and training they need to explore new ideas. Consider offering access to workshops, online courses, or seminars that align with the team's interests and goals. These resources equip team members with the skills and knowledge to turn their ideas into reality. Additionally, allocating time for creative pursuits is vital. This might involve setting aside regular "innovation hours" where team members can focus on projects outside their typical responsibilities. By making time for creativity, you acknowledge that innovation doesn't always fit into traditional work hours and that it requires dedicated attention and focus.

Learning from failures is an integral part of the innovation process. In a culture that values growth, failures are seen not as setbacks, but as opportunities for learning and improvement. Promoting a mindset where team members feel safe to experiment and fail is key. Debrief sessions focusing on lessons learned from unsuccessful attempts can provide valuable insights. These sessions should aim to analyze what went wrong, what could be improved, and how similar challenges can be approached differently in the future. Sharing case studies of successful recoveries from failures can further illustrate the potential for growth and resilience. These stories demonstrate that failure isn't the end but a step in the journey toward success. By normalizing failure as part of the creative process, you empower your team to take risks without fear, knowing that each attempt, successful or not, contributes to their development and the organization's progress.

5.4 MANAGING DIVERSE TEAM DYNAMICS

Understanding team diversity is a multifaceted endeavor, encompassing a wide range of dimensions, from cultural and ethnic backgrounds to diverse experiences and perspectives. Each team member brings a unique set of values, beliefs, and skills to the table, and recognizing these contributions is crucial to harnessing the full potential of your team. Engaging in cultural competence training is a valuable starting point. This training helps team members understand and appreciate the diverse backgrounds that influence how individuals approach problem-solving and collaboration. By developing cultural competence, you create an environment where diversity is seen as a strength, not a challenge. Diversity mapping exercises can further illuminate these dynamics, offering a visual representation of the varied identities and competencies within your team. These exercises highlight gaps or imbalances and celebrate the rich tapestry of experiences that can drive innovation and creativity.

Conflicts often arise from diverse perspectives, but addressing them constructively can transform potential friction into opportunities for growth. Mediation techniques serve as a practical tool in these situations, offering a structured approach to resolving disagreements. By facilitating open dialogue and encouraging active listening, mediation allows team members to express their viewpoints and find common ground. Conflict resolution frameworks provide additional support, offering step-by-step guidance on navigating disputes. These frameworks emphasize collaboration, focusing on shared goals rather than individual differences. Implementing these strategies resolves conflicts effectively and strengthens relationships within the team, creating a more cohesive and resilient group. By viewing conflicts as natural and even beneficial, you can foster a culture where diverse perspectives are not just tolerated, but actively sought out and valued.

Leveraging diversity for innovation is not merely a possibility—it is a proven strategy that can significantly enhance creativity and problem-solving. Diverse teams bring a wealth of ideas and approaches to the table, challenging conventional thinking and fostering innovative solutions. Cross-functional team projects exemplify this potential. By bringing together individuals from different departments or areas of expertise, these projects encourage collaboration beyond traditional boundaries. Innovation workshops, which highlight diverse ideas and approaches, can further stimulate creative thinking. These workshops provide a platform for team members to share and refine their ideas, drawing on the collective wisdom of the group. By prioritizing diversity in team composition and project planning, you can unlock new levels of innovation and creativity, driving success for your team and organization.

Creating inclusive team norms is vital to ensuring that all members feel respected and valued for their contributions. Establishing a team charter with inclusivity clauses can serve as a foundational document that outlines the team's commitment to diversity and inclusion. This charter should reflect the team's values and goals, providing a clear framework for behavior and decision-making. Norm-setting workshops offer an interactive opportunity to develop these guidelines collectively, ensuring buy-in from all team members. During these workshops, encourage open discussion about what inclusivity means to the team and how it can be implemented in daily interactions. By involving everyone in the process, you create a sense of ownership and accountability for maintaining these norms. This inclusive approach strengthens the team's commitment to diversity and enables a supportive environment where all voices are heard and valued.

5.5 BUILDING TRUST AND COLLABORATION AMONG TEAM MEMBERS

Trust is the bedrock of effective teamwork. It's built through consistency, where your actions align with your words, creating reliability. When you consistently follow through on commitments, you demonstrate respect for your team's time and efforts. This predictability fosters confidence, allowing team members to feel secure in their roles and interactions. Consistency in leadership doesn't mean rigidity, but rather reliability in your actions and decisions. It's about being dependable in delivering what you promise, thereby setting a standard that encourages others to do the same. This foundation of trust becomes the glue that holds a high-performing team together, enabling them to navigate challenges with cohesion and resilience.

Team-building activities are instrumental in strengthening the bonds between team members. These activities provide an informal setting where individuals can connect on a personal level, beyond their professional roles. Organizing team retreats or offsite workshops can be particularly effective in this regard. These settings allow team members to step away from the usual pressures of the workplace and engage in collaborative projects or challenges that require them to rely on one another. Through shared experiences, such as problem-solving exercises or outdoor adventures, team members develop a deeper understanding of each other's strengths and personalities. This understanding fosters empathy and appreciation, key ingredients for collaboration. By investing in these activities, you create opportunities for team members to build lasting relationships, which translate into more effective and harmonious teamwork back at the office.

Aligning team members around shared goals and vision is crucial for achieving collective success. When everyone is working towards the same objectives, collaboration becomes natural and purposeful. Goal-setting sessions provide a platform for discussing and defining these objectives, ensuring that each team member understands their role in the larger mission. During these sessions, encourage open dialogue about individual and team goals, aligning them with the organization's vision. Vision board exercises can be a creative way to visualize these goals, making them tangible and inspiring. By having a visual representation of the collective aspirations, team members can see how their efforts contribute to the bigger picture. This alignment motivates individuals and ensures a sense of ownership and accountability, driving the team's progress toward shared success.

A culture of recognition plays a significant role in building trust and collaboration. When team members feel appreciated for their contributions, they are more likely to engage and invest in their work and relationships with colleagues. Peer-to-peer recognition programs encourage team members to acknowledge each other's efforts, creating a positive feedback loop that reinforces collaborative behavior. Platforms for sharing accolades, such as internal newsletters or digital boards, can highlight these recognitions, making achievements visible across the organization. This visibility boosts morale and sets a standard for excellence and teamwork. By celebrating successes and recognizing the contributions of each member, you cultivate an environment where everyone feels valued and motivated to collaborate. This culture of appreciation strengthens the bonds between team members, enhancing their ability to work together towards common goals.

Building trust and collaboration within a team requires ongoing effort and attention. It's about creating an environment where team members feel supported and empowered to contribute their best. As you focus on consistency, facilitate team-building activities, align shared goals, and encourage peer recognition, you lay the groundwork for a cohesive and high-performing team.

5.6 OVERCOMING CHALLENGES IN BUILDING INCLUSIVE TEAMS

Building inclusive teams is not a straightforward task. It begins with recognizing barriers that may hinder inclusivity. Often, these obstacles are deeply embedded in workplace culture, making them difficult to identify without a conscious effort. Surveys can be a practical method to spotlight inclusivity gaps. By asking direct questions, you can uncover areas where employees feel excluded or unheard. These surveys should be anonymous to encourage honesty. But numbers only tell part of the story. To gain deeper insights, focus groups can be instrumental. These discussions allow team members to express their thoughts in a supportive environment, shedding light on specific challenges and potential solutions. Through these conversations, themes often emerge, revealing systemic issues that need addressing.

Implementing inclusive practices requires actionable steps. Inclusive hiring practices are a foundational element. By casting a wider net during recruitment, you bring in diverse perspectives that enrich team dynamics. This means not just looking at traditional qualifications, but considering potential and diverse experiences. Beyond hiring, diverse representation in leadership roles is crucial. It's about seeing leaders who reflect the diversity of the team, providing role models and ensuring that different voices are heard at decision-making tables. This representation can inspire confidence and offer varied perspectives, which are essential for tackling complex challenges. By prioritizing diversity in leadership, you send a clear message that inclusivity is valued at all levels.

Education on unconscious bias is another significant step. Biases often shape interactions and decisions without our awareness, affecting team dynamics and inclusivity. Bias training workshops can help team members recognize these biases and understand their impact. These workshops often include activities that highlight how biases manifest in everyday situations, encouraging participants to reflect on their behaviors. Implicit bias assessments can further individual understanding, providing a baseline from which to grow. By raising awareness, you empower individuals to challenge their assumptions and make more informed, equitable decisions. This education fosters a culture of self-awareness and responsibility, crucial for sustaining inclusive practices.

Celebrating multiculturalism and diversity is also important. It's not enough to acknowledge diversity; it must be actively celebrated. Cultural exchange events can be a vibrant way to showcase different backgrounds and traditions within the team. These events can include food, music, and storytelling, offering team members a chance to learn from one another. These celebrations highlight the richness of diversity and strengthen bonds within the team. Diversity appreciation days can further reinforce the importance of inclusivity. These days can focus on recognizing contributions from team members of various backgrounds, promoting a sense of belonging and appreciation. By creating opportunities to celebrate diversity, you cultivate an environment where everyone feels valued and respected.

In the pursuit of inclusivity, it's crucial to remember that challenges are opportunities for growth. Each barrier overcome strengthens the team, making it more resilient and innovative. As leaders, your role is to guide this process, ensuring that inclusivity is not just a goal, but a reality. By identifying barriers, implementing inclusive practices, educating on bias, and celebrating diversity, you lay the foundation for a team that thrives on collaboration and mutual respect. This approach benefits the team and enhances the organization's ability to adapt and succeed in a diverse world.

As we conclude this chapter, remember that inclusivity is another ongoing commitment. It's about creating an environment where every voice is heard and valued, nurturing a culture of acceptance and respect. Moving forward, continue to champion diversity and inclusion, ensuring that your team is not only diverse in makeup but also in thought and action!

SKILL #6 - BALANCING PROFESSIONAL AND PERSONAL LIFE

I magine this: an email notification pings just as you're about to step out for a family dinner. The tug-of-war between professional obligations and personal commitments is too familiar. As female leaders, you often find yourself standing at the intersection of work demands and personal aspirations. Balancing these spheres isn't just about managing time, but about crafting a life where both can thrive harmoniously. This chapter dives into the art of time management, providing you with tools to navigate this delicate balance with grace and intention.

6.1 TIME MANAGEMENT FOR BUSY LEADERS

Particularly in leadership, time is an invaluable currency. To manage it effectively, distinguishing between tasks that are urgent and those that are important is crucial. The Eisenhower Matrix, a tool rooted in the wisdom of former President Dwight D. Eisenhower, offers a framework for prioritizing tasks based on their urgency and importance. This method organizes your workload and aligns your daily actions with long-term goals, enhancing productivity and focus. By implementing this strategy, you can ensure that your time is spent on tasks that truly matter, rather than being consumed by the tyranny of the urgent.

Interactive Exercise: Learning the Eisenhower Matrix

Start by categorizing tasks into four quadrants, in order to streamline your decision-making process:

- Quadrant 1: Urgent and important - Do these tasks first. These require your immediate attention.
- Quadrant 2: Urgent but not important - Delegate these tasks as best as you can.
- Quadrant 3: Not urgent but important: - Schedule these tasks for a later time.
- Quadrant 4: Not urgent and not important - Delete these tasks from your schedule for the day.

Adopting this matrix simplifies decision-making by helping you focus on what truly drives progress while avoiding the trap of busywork. This clear categorization empowers you to allocate your time and resources more efficiently, ensuring that your daily actions contribute meaningfully to your long-term objectives.

Also, consider adopting daily priority setting routines to maintain clarity and direction. Begin each day by identifying the top three tasks that align most closely with your goals. This practice ensures that your efforts are concentrated on tasks that drive meaningful progress. Incorporating tools like color-coded schedules or digital task lists can further enhance your organizational prowess. These routines create a structured approach to your day, reducing mental clutter and allowing you to approach each task with renewed focus and energy. Over time, these small adjustments accumulate, transforming your approach to time management and increasing your overall effectiveness as a leader.

Time blocking is another powerful technique that can revolutionize how you manage your schedule. By allocating specific time slots for different activities, you create a structured environment that minimizes distractions and enhances productivity. This method involves dividing your day into blocks, with each dedicated to a specific task or group of tasks. Time blocking not only provides a clear structure, but also boosts your focus by ensuring that each task receives your undivided attention. Examples of effective time-blocking schedules might include dedicating mornings to strategic planning, afternoons to meetings, and late afternoons to creative pursuits. This approach ensures that each aspect of your role receives the attention it deserves, ultimately leading to more efficient and effective work.

To further enhance your time management skills, consider utilizing productivity tools and apps. Digital platforms like Trello, Asana, or Todoist can be instrumental in organizing tasks and projects. These apps allow you to create task lists, set deadlines, and collaborate with team members, all in one place. By integrating these tools into your daily routine, you gain a comprehensive overview of your workload, enabling you to prioritize tasks and allocate resources effectively. These platforms also offer features like reminders and notifications, ensuring that important tasks are never overlooked. Embracing technology in this way streamlines your workflow and provides the flexibility to adapt to changing demands.

Identifying and eliminating time-wasters is another key aspect of effective time management. Begin by conducting a time audit to assess how you currently spend your days. This process involves tracking your activities over a period of time to identify patterns and areas where time might be slipping away unnoticed. Once you've identified these areas, implement strategies to reduce distractions and minimize non-essential activities. Simple changes, such as setting boundaries around email usage or designating specific times for social media, can have a significant impact on your productivity. By consciously addressing these time-wasters, you create space for more meaningful and impactful work, allowing you to lead with greater focus and efficiency.

Reflective Element: Conducting a Time Audit

- **Step 1**: Track your activities for one week using a journal or a digital tool.
- **Step 2**: Categorize each activity by its purpose and duration.
- **Step 3**: Identify patterns and areas where time is often wasted.
- **Step 4**: Develop strategies to minimize these time-wasters and reallocate time to more productive tasks.

Embarking on this journey of time management equips you with the tools to lead effectively, balancing professional responsibilities with personal aspirations. By implementing these strategies, you optimize your schedule and create a life where both work and personal pursuits can flourish.

6.2 SETTING BOUNDARIES TO PREVENT BURNOUT

In the whirlwind of leadership, burnout can stealthily creep up, manifesting as chronic fatigue, irritability, or a sense of detachment from work. Recognizing these early signs allows you to take preventive action before burnout takes hold. Pay attention to physical and emotional exhaustion, and notice if you feel overwhelmed by tasks that once inspired you. These indicators are your body's way of signaling that it needs a pause. Ignoring them can lead to more severe consequences, not just affecting productivity but also your overall well-being. By staying attuned to these signals, you can implement strategies that protect your health and sustain your leadership effectiveness.

Establishing clear work-life boundaries is a fundamental step in preventing burnout. It starts with mastering the art of saying "no" to tasks or commitments that overextend you. This doesn't mean closing off opportunities; rather, it's about choosing where to focus your energy. Practice assertive communication that respects both your limits and the demands of your role. End-of-day rituals can also help you disconnect from work, providing a mental cue that it's time to transition into personal life. Whether it's shutting down your computer, engaging in a hobby, or spending time with loved ones, these rituals create a buffer that separates work from home. Regularly practicing these habits reinforces a healthy boundary, ensuring you're not constantly in work mode, even when you're off the clock.

Communicating your boundaries to colleagues and family is equally crucial. It's important to set expectations about your availability and the times you are off-limits for work-related issues. Drafting boundary communication templates can serve as a guide. These templates help articulate your needs clearly and respectfully, whether in an email to a colleague or a conversation with a family member. For instance, you might explain that you do not respond to work emails after a certain hour to prioritize family time. Establishing these parameters requires consistency and clarity, so others know when you are accessible and when you need uninterrupted personal time.

Boundaries are not static; they require regular reassessment to remain effective. As your role evolves, so should your boundaries. Adapt to new responsibilities and personal needs by periodically reviewing these boundaries to ensure they still align with your current goals and commitments. A boundary reassessment checklist can be a useful tool, prompting you to reflect on what's working and what needs adjustment. Consider questions like: Are there new stressors in your role that require additional boundaries? Have your personal priorities shifted, necessitating a different approach? This reflective practice helps you maintain balance and empowers you to take proactive control over your work-life integration.

Setting and maintaining boundaries is not just about drawing lines but about cultivating a lifestyle that supports your well-being. By recognizing the signs of burnout and taking intentional steps to create and communicate boundaries, you safeguard your energy and focus. This approach not only enhances your professional performance, but also enriches your personal life, allowing you to be fully present in both areas.

6.3 PRIORITIZING SELF-CARE AND PERSONAL WELL-BEING

In the hustle and bustle of daily life, self-care often takes a backseat. Yet, it is a vital component of maintaining both personal health and professional effectiveness. Integrating self-care into daily routines is not just beneficial; it is necessary. Start your day with morning routines centered on mindfulness. These moments of calm can set a positive tone for the day. Whether it's a few minutes of meditation, a quiet cup of coffee, or a mindful walk, these practices ground you and prepare you for the challenges ahead. As the day winds down, evening rituals provide a chance to reflect and release the day's stress. Whether it's reading a book, practicing gratitude journaling, or engaging in light stretches, these activities help transition your mind from work mode to rest, promoting better sleep and relaxation.

Exploring various self-care practices allows you to find what resonates with you personally. For some, yoga and meditation offer a path to inner peace and physical well-being. These practices not only enhance flexibility and strength, but also facilitate mental clarity and stress reduction. Engaging in creative outlets like art or music can also serve as a powerful form of self-care. Whether it's painting, writing, playing an instrument, or even crafting, these activities provide an escape from the pressures of leadership and a chance to express yourself freely. They activate different parts of the brain, encouraging creativity and problem-solving. Engaging in these practices regularly can rejuvenate your spirit and provide fresh perspectives, making you more adaptable and resilient in your leadership role.

Scheduling regular self-care time is a commitment to your well-being that pays dividends in productivity and focus. Consider blocking off "self-care Sundays" or a specific time during the week dedicated solely to activities that replenish your energy. This scheduled time acts as a non-negotiable appointment with yourself, ensuring that self-care remains a priority amidst other responsibilities. By treating this time with the same importance as a business meeting, you reinforce its value in your life. This regular practice recharges your mental and physical energy and enhances your ability to tackle challenges with renewed vigor and creativity. The consistency of this routine builds a habit that integrates self-care seamlessly into your lifestyle, making it an integral part of your overall well-being strategy.

The impact of self-care on productivity is profound. Prioritizing well-being enhances focus and effectiveness, leading to improved work performance. Research shows that individuals who engage in regular self-care practices often report higher levels of satisfaction and achievement in both personal and professional arenas. By investing in self-care, you are not merely indulging in a luxury; you are laying the foundation for sustained success. This investment in yourself fosters a positive mindset, reducing stress and preventing burnout. It allows you to approach your work with clarity and purpose, driving productivity and innovation. As you cultivate a balanced approach to work and life, you create an environment where both can flourish without compromising either.

6.4 STRATEGIES FOR EFFECTIVE DELEGATION

Delegation can transform how you manage your responsibilities and empower your team. The first step is identifying which tasks can be delegated. Not every task requires your direct involvement, and knowing which ones to pass on is critical. A delegation matrix can help evaluate tasks based on complexity, importance, and the skill level required. This tool categorizes tasks into those you must handle personally, those you can delegate to experienced team members, and those suitable for development opportunities. By leveraging this matrix, you can focus on high-impact activities while developing your team's capabilities and confidence.

Choosing the right person for each task is just as important as deciding what to delegate. Start by understanding your team members' strengths and areas for growth. This insight allows you to match tasks with individuals who have the right skills and potential. Consider their workloads and interests, as well. Delegating tasks aligned with a team member's strengths and career aspirations ensures the task is completed effectively and boosts morale and engagement. This approach creates a win-win scenario, where tasks are efficiently managed, and team members feel valued and challenged in their roles.

Once you've identified the tasks and team members, setting clear expectations is essential. Providing detailed instructions and context is key. This might involve creating comprehensive project briefs that outline objectives, deadlines, and deliverables. Clarity in communication prevents misunderstandings and sets a standard for accountability. It also empowers your team to take ownership of their work, knowing exactly what's expected of them. When team members understand the bigger picture and their role within it, they are more likely to contribute meaningfully and innovate within their tasks. Open communication throughout the project lifecycle reinforces this understanding and keeps everyone aligned.

Monitoring progress without micromanaging is a delicate balance to strike. Regular check-in meetings offer a structured yet flexible way to touch base with your team. These meetings should focus on providing support and guidance rather than oversight. Encourage team members to share updates, challenges, and successes. This fosters a collaborative environment where everyone feels comfortable seeking help and offering solutions. Additionally, using project management tools can streamline this process. These platforms provide real-time updates on task progress, deadlines, and team collaboration, allowing you to stay informed without hovering over every detail. By reinforcing a culture of trust and accountability, you enable your team to thrive, enhancing overall productivity and effectiveness.

Delegation is not just about offloading tasks; it's about empowering your team to contribute their best while freeing you to focus on strategic initiatives. As you refine your delegation skills, you'll find that it not only improves workflow, but also strengthens your team's capabilities and confidence. This collective growth benefits everyone, creating a dynamic and responsive work environment. Through thoughtful delegation, you can achieve more, support your team's development, and lead with greater impact and efficiency.

6.5 CULTIVATING A GROWTH MINDSET FOR BALANCE

In both leadership and life, the mindset you embrace can profoundly affect your ability to balance professional and personal commitments. Understanding the concept of a growth mindset is essential for fostering this balance. Unlike a fixed mindset, which assumes abilities and intelligence are static, a growth mindset thrives on the belief that these qualities can be developed through dedication and hard work. This perspective opens doors for continuous improvement, viewing challenges not as threats but as opportunities to learn and grow. Adopting a growth mindset means welcoming feedback and change, using them to fuel personal and professional development. This approach encourages you to embrace possibilities, expanding your capacity to manage the complexities of leadership with resilience and adaptability.

Viewing work-life balance challenges as opportunities for growth transforms potential obstacles into stepping stones. Consider the story of a manager who, upon realizing the strain her work was placing on her family, took it as a chance to reassess her priorities. By setting clearer boundaries and focusing on what's truly important, she found a new equilibrium that enhanced both her work performance and personal satisfaction. These challenges, when approached with a growth mindset, become catalysts for positive change. They prompt you to explore creative solutions, develop new skills, and strengthen your ability to adapt, ultimately enriching your experience in both spheres.

Promoting lifelong learning and adaptability is another cornerstone of achieving balance. The ever-evolving nature of work and life demands continuous learning and flexibility. Enrolling in courses or workshops can expand your knowledge and skills, keeping you abreast of new developments and practices. Whether it's a leadership seminar, a technical course, or a creative workshop, these learning experiences enhance your professional capabilities and stimulate personal growth. Reading and reflecting on new ideas further contribute to this process. Engaging with diverse perspectives broadens your understanding, sparking innovation and inspiring fresh approaches to familiar challenges. This commitment to learning fosters a mindset that is open to change and equipped to handle the unpredictability of work-life dynamics.

Resilience is a vital trait that helps you weather the setbacks and disruptions that inevitably arise. Building resilience involves developing strategies to manage stress and maintain focus during challenging times. Techniques like mindfulness and stress management can be particularly effective. Mindfulness encourages you to stay present, reducing anxiety and enhancing clarity. Practices such as meditation or deep breathing exercises can ground you, providing a sense of calm amid chaos. Stress management techniques, including physical exercise, time in nature, or engaging in hobbies, help release tension and recharge your energy. These practices bolster your resilience and reinforce your ability to maintain balance, allowing you to respond to disruptions with composure and confidence.

By cultivating a growth mindset, you create a foundation for navigating life's complexities with agility and insight. This mindset empowers you to see beyond immediate challenges, envisioning a path where personal and professional aspirations coexist harmoniously. The journey toward balance becomes less about perfection and more about progress, embracing each step as a valuable part of your growth. In this way, you enhance your effectiveness as a leader and enrich your overall well-being, creating a life that is both fulfilling and sustainable.

6.6 LEVERAGING TECHNOLOGY FOR WORK-LIFE INTEGRATION

In today's digital age, technology offers a myriad of tools designed to streamline tasks and simplify our busy lives. Imagine having a virtual assistant that automates your scheduling, manages reminders, or even organizes your emails. These tools, such as Google Calendar or Microsoft Outlook, allow you to automate routine tasks, leaving you free to focus on more pressing matters. Tools like these can sync across devices, ensuring that your schedule is always up-to-date and accessible, whether you're at your desk or on the go. By automating repetitive tasks, you reduce the mental load, freeing up cognitive resources for strategic thinking and decision-making.

Remote work solutions are great tools to use to your advantage, enabling flexible work arrangements that support a balanced lifestyle. Platforms like Zoom and Microsoft Teams facilitate seamless virtual meetings, allowing you to collaborate with colleagues and clients from anywhere in the world. These tools reduce the need for travel and offer flexible working hours, accommodating personal commitments and preferences. The ability to work remotely can be a game-changer, providing opportunities to design a work-life balance that suits your unique needs. By embracing remote work, you can eliminate the constraints of a traditional office, creating a more adaptable and responsive work environment.

However, the same technology that enhances productivity can also blur the lines between work and personal life. Setting digital boundaries is essential to prevent work from intruding on your personal time. Consider setting notifications and screen time limits on your devices to ensure that work-related alerts don't interrupt your downtime. Apps like Forest or Focus@Will can help maintain focus during work hours while encouraging breaks to recharge. By establishing clear boundaries, you protect your personal time, ensuring that technology serves as a tool for balance rather than a source of constant connection. This discipline helps maintain a healthy separation between professional responsibilities and personal relaxation.

Enhancing collaboration with digital tools is another way technology can support both individual and team productivity. Platforms like Slack and Basecamp facilitate communication and project management, allowing teams to collaborate efficiently even when working remotely. These tools offer features such as real-time messaging, file sharing, and task management, centralizing all communication in one place. By using these platforms, teams can stay connected, share updates, and coordinate efforts seamlessly, regardless of geographical location. This connectivity boosts team efficiency and fosters a sense of community and collaboration, making remote work more cohesive and productive.

As technology continues to evolve, its role in work-life integration becomes increasingly pivotal. By leveraging these tools thoughtfully, you can design a lifestyle that accommodates professional demands while honoring personal commitments. This integration empowers you to lead with flexibility and intention, creating a harmonious balance that enhances both work performance and personal fulfillment.

In this chapter, we've explored the transformative potential of technology in crafting a balanced life. From streamlining tasks to enabling remote work and maintaining digital boundaries, these tools offer a framework for integrating professional and personal realms. As we move forward, we will delve into how these strategies can cultivate trust and collaboration, enhancing your leadership impact and effectiveness.

SKILL #7 - DEVELOPING A DYNAMIC LEADERSHIP STYLE

Imagine a symphony orchestra preparing for a grand performance. Each musician tunes their instrument, the conductor raises their baton, and the room fills with anticipation. Much like this orchestra, effective leadership requires harmony, with each strength playing its part in a well-conducted symphony. Developing a dynamic leadership style begins with understanding the unique strengths that each team member brings to the table. Identifying these strengths is akin to tuning your instrument, ensuring that it resonates beautifully within the larger organizational context.

7.1 DISCOVERING YOUR LEADERSHIP STYLE

Start by assessing your personal and professional strengths. This self-discovery process is essential for crafting a leadership style that is both authentic and effective. Strength assessment tools, such as the CliftonStrengths or VIA Survey, can provide valuable insights into your innate talents and capabilities. These tools offer a structured approach to uncovering what you naturally excel at, whether it be strategic thinking, relationship building, or influencing others. However, self-assessment is only part of the equation. Feedback from peers and mentors can further illuminate strengths you might not have recognized. Engaging in regular feedback sessions allows for a comprehensive view of your leadership capabilities, revealing strengths that others observe in your day-to-day interactions.

Once you've identified your core strengths, it's time to explore how these align with various leadership styles. Leadership is not a one-size-fits-all endeavor. Different styles resonate with different strengths, and understanding these can help you find your unique approach. Transformational leadership, for example, is well-suited for those who are visionary and excel in motivating others toward a common goal. Transactional leadership, on the other hand, is effective for those who thrive in structured environments and are skilled in setting clear expectations and rewards. Servant leadership appeals to those who prioritize the needs of their team and focus on personal growth and community building. By exploring these styles, you can identify which aligns most closely with your strengths, allowing you to lead in a way that feels natural and effective.

Creating a personalized leadership style blueprint is the next step in developing a dynamic leadership style. This blueprint serves as a roadmap, guiding your actions and decisions in alignment with your strengths and chosen leadership style. Consider using templates that outline key components such as your leadership vision, goals, and strategies for leveraging strengths. This structured approach ensures that your leadership style is intentional, but also adaptable, to evolving circumstances. As you draft your blueprint, reflect on past experiences and lessons learned, incorporating these insights into your leadership strategy. This process transforms abstract concepts into actionable plans, allowing for a leadership style that is both dynamic and grounded in reality.

Aligning your strengths with organizational goals is crucial for maximizing your impact as a leader. When your personal strengths resonate with the mission and objectives of the organization, you create a synergy that drives success. Consider case studies of leaders who have effectively aligned their strengths with organizational goals. For instance, a leader with a talent for innovation might spearhead a project focused on developing cutting-edge solutions, directly contributing to the company's growth strategy. By aligning your strengths with the overarching goals of your organization, you enhance your effectiveness and contribute to a culture of achievement and collaboration. This alignment ensures that your leadership is impactful and that your contributions are recognized and valued within the organization.

Interactive Exercise: Leadership Style Blueprint Template

- **Vision Statement**: Define your long-term leadership vision and how it aligns with your core strengths.
- **Goals**: Identify specific goals related to your leadership development and organizational objectives.
- **Strategies**: Outline strategies for leveraging your strengths in various leadership scenarios.
- **Feedback Integration**: Include a plan for incorporating regular feedback from peers and mentors to refine your approach.

By embracing your unique strengths and aligning them with a leadership style that complements both your personality and organizational goals, you can develop a dynamic leadership style that empowers you and inspires those around you.

7.2 EMBRACING FLEXIBILITY AND ADAPTABILITY IN LEADERSHIP

In the fast-paced and ever-evolving landscape of today's work environment, adaptability has emerged as a cornerstone of effective leadership. Industries are changing at unprecedented rates, driven by technological advancements, shifting consumer preferences, and global disruptions. Leaders who can pivot and adjust to these changes not only survive, but thrive. Consider the rapid evolution in the technology sector, where companies must constantly innovate to remain competitive. Here, adaptability is not just an advantage—it's a necessity. Leaders who embrace change and adjust their strategies accordingly keep their teams agile and ready to tackle new challenges. This ability to adapt is crucial for maintaining relevance and effectiveness in any field.

Developing adaptive thinking skills is key to navigating this dynamic terrain. Cognitive flexibility allows leaders to approach problems from multiple angles, fostering innovation and creativity. Participating in lateral thinking exercises is a powerful method to bolster adaptive thinking. These exercises challenge individuals to step outside traditional thought processes and investigate a wide array of solutions to any given problem. By doing so, leaders can discover unconventional and innovative approaches that might have been overlooked. These activities can range from simple brainstorming sessions that push for rapid idea generation without immediate judgment, to complex scenario planning exercises that require imagining multiple futures and determining possible responses. Engaging in these exercises on a regular basis not only refines a leader's problem-solving skills but also instills a culture of creativity and openness within the team.

Problem-solving workshops further provide a structured environment to practice these skills, offering scenarios that require quick thinking and adaptability. By regularly participating in such activities, you sharpen your ability to respond to unexpected challenges with agility and confidence. This proactive approach to problem-solving ensures that you are prepared for whatever comes your way.

Open-mindedness is another vital aspect of adaptability. Remaining open to new ideas and perspectives allows leaders to harness the collective intelligence of their teams. It involves creating a culture where team members feel encouraged to share their thoughts and suggestions without fear of judgment. Techniques for nurturing open-mindedness include welcoming diverse viewpoints during brainstorming sessions and actively seeking feedback from all levels of the organization. By valuing different perspectives, you enhance your decision-making process and empower your team to contribute meaningfully. This inclusive approach fosters a collaborative environment where innovation and adaptability go hand in hand.

Promoting a culture of adaptability within your team is essential for navigating the complexities of today's work environment. Encouraging team members to embrace change and view challenges as opportunities for growth cultivates a resilient and flexible team dynamic. Implementing team adaptability challenges can be an effective way to instill this mindset. These challenges might involve cross-functional projects that require team members to step outside their usual roles and collaborate on new initiatives. Flexibility in project management further supports this culture, allowing teams to pivot and adjust their strategies as needed. By embedding adaptability into the fabric of your team's operations, you create a robust foundation for continuous improvement and success.

In a world where change is the only constant, embracing flexibility and adaptability in leadership is not an option; it's a requirement. Leaders who cultivate these qualities enhance their own effectiveness and inspire their teams to reach new heights. The ability to adapt and thrive in the face of uncertainty is what sets successful leaders apart, ensuring their continued growth and success in any environment.

7.3 NAVIGATING CHANGE AND UNCERTAINTY WITH CONFIDENCE

Preparing for organizational change requires a proactive mindset and strategic planning. Anticipating changes within an organization means staying informed about industry trends and internal developments. Utilizing change management frameworks can guide you in structuring the transition process. These frameworks often include steps like assessing the current state, defining the desired future state, and developing a comprehensive plan to bridge the gap. It's important to involve key stakeholders early in the process to gather diverse perspectives and ensure a holistic approach. By mapping out potential challenges and opportunities ahead of time, you can create a roadmap that prepares you for change and positions your team to thrive in new environments.

Resilience becomes a vital asset during times of uncertainty. It's about more than just bouncing back; it involves growing through adversity and emerging stronger. Developing resilience requires intentional effort and practice. Storytelling is another effective tool for building resilience—sharing narratives of past experiences where you successfully navigated uncertainty can reinforce your ability to handle future challenges. For instance, consider recounting a time when you faced a major organizational shift, detailing the steps you took to adapt and the lessons learned. This reflection boosts your confidence and serves as a guide for others facing similar situations.

Effective communication is crucial during periods of change. Transparent communication helps maintain trust and morale within your team. Crisis communication plans can provide a structured approach to delivering clear and consistent messages. These plans outline the key points to address, the channels to use, and the timing of communications. Messaging templates can ensure that the information is conveyed uniformly, reducing misunderstandings. It's important to communicate openly about the reasons for change, the expected impact, and the support available to team members. By being upfront and honest, you create a sense of security and stability, even amidst uncertainty.

Leading by example during uncertain times is perhaps the most powerful way to inspire your team. Demonstrating calm and confidence provides reassurance and sets the tone for how the team responds. Look to profiles of leaders who have successfully navigated change. Leaders like Indra Nooyi, former CEO of PepsiCo, are known for their ability to guide their organizations through transitions while maintaining a strong vision. Their composure and strategic foresight serve as models for effective leadership. By embodying these qualities, you not only guide your team through change, but also create an environment where adaptability and resilience are part of the organizational culture.

7.4 INSPIRING AND LEADING BY EXAMPLE

The impact of leading by example cannot be understated. A leader's actions and behaviors are powerful signals that set the tone for the entire team. When leaders embody the values and work ethic they wish to see in others, they inspire a culture of trust and integrity. History is filled with examples of leaders who have left indelible marks on their organizations and communities through their exemplary conduct. Consider Mahatma Gandhi, whose principle of non-violence and commitment to peace inspired millions to follow his lead, not through coercion but through the sheer power of example. These leaders demonstrate how consistently living their values can galvanize others to strive for a common goal, creating an environment where morale and performance thrive.

To effectively model desired behaviors, leaders must first identify the values and practices they wish to see reflected in their teams. This requires a conscious effort to align personal conduct with organizational objectives. Role-playing exercises can be particularly useful in this context, allowing leaders to practice and refine the behaviors they aim to promote. These exercises simulate real-world scenarios where leaders can demonstrate empathy, decisiveness, and collaboration, providing a clear blueprint for team members to emulate. By consistently exhibiting these behaviors, leaders reinforce their expectations and foster an atmosphere of mutual respect and accountability.

Communicating a clear vision and purpose is vital to inspire and engage a team. When leaders articulate a compelling vision, they provide a sense of direction and meaning that motivates individuals to contribute their best efforts. Vision statement development workshops can aid in crafting a vision that resonates with both the leader and the team, ensuring that it aligns with organizational goals and personal values. These workshops encourage introspection and dialogue, helping leaders crystallize their aspirations and communicate them effectively. A well-communicated vision acts as a guiding star, aligning team efforts and inspiring collective action toward a shared future.

Recognizing and celebrating team contributions is a cornerstone of effective leadership. Acknowledging the achievements of team members not only boosts morale, but also reinforces a culture of appreciation and motivation. Recognition programs and events provide formal avenues for celebrating successes, whether through awards, public commendations, or team celebrations. Personalized appreciation notes can also have a profound impact, offering a more intimate form of recognition that highlights individual contributions. These notes convey genuine gratitude and acknowledgment, strengthening the bond between leaders and their teams. By celebrating achievements, leaders show that every effort counts, fostering a sense of belonging and pride within the team.

Leaders who inspire by example, communicate vision with clarity, and celebrate contributions create a vibrant and cohesive team environment. This approach enhances individual performance and cultivates a collective spirit of excellence and innovation. As leaders embody the principles they advocate, they empower others to follow suit, building a legacy of trust, respect, and achievement.

7.4 INSPIRING AND LEADING BY EXAMPLE

The impact of leading by example cannot be understated. A leader's actions and behaviors are powerful signals that set the tone for the entire team. When leaders embody the values and work ethic they wish to see in others, they inspire a culture of trust and integrity. History is filled with examples of leaders who have left indelible marks on their organizations and communities through their exemplary conduct. Consider Malala Yousafzai, whose unwavering commitment to education, even in the face of life-threatening danger, inspired millions around the world. By continuing her advocacy for female education after surviving an assassination attempt, she exemplifies courage, resilience, and dedication to a cause greater than herself. Such leaders demonstrate how consistently living their values can galvanize others to strive for a common goal, creating an environment where morale and performance thrive.

To effectively model desired behaviors, leaders must first identify the values and practices they wish to see reflected in their teams. This requires a conscious effort to align personal conduct with organizational objectives. Role-playing exercises can be particularly useful in this context, allowing leaders to practice and refine the behaviors they aim to promote. These exercises simulate real-world scenarios where leaders can demonstrate empathy, decisiveness, and collaboration, providing a clear blueprint for team members to emulate. By consistently exhibiting these behaviors, leaders reinforce their expectations and foster an atmosphere of mutual respect and accountability.

Communicating a clear vision and purpose is vital to inspire and engage a team. When leaders articulate a compelling vision, they provide a sense of direction and meaning that motivates individuals to contribute their best efforts. Vision statement development workshops can aid in crafting a vision that resonates with both the leader and the team, ensuring that it aligns with organizational goals and personal values. These workshops encourage introspection and dialogue, helping leaders crystallize their aspirations and communicate them effectively. A well-communicated vision acts as a guiding star, aligning team efforts and inspiring collective action toward a shared future.

Recognizing and celebrating team contributions is a cornerstone of effective leadership. Acknowledging the achievements of team members not only boosts morale but also reinforces a culture of appreciation and motivation. Recognition programs and events provide formal avenues for celebrating successes, whether through awards, public commendations, or team celebrations. Personalized appreciation notes can also have a profound impact, offering a more intimate form of recognition that highlights individual contributions. These notes convey genuine gratitude and acknowledgment, strengthening the bond between leaders and their teams. By celebrating achievements, leaders show that every effort counts, fostering a sense of belonging and pride within the team.

Leaders who inspire by example, communicate vision with clarity, and celebrate contributions create a vibrant and cohesive team environment. This approach not only enhances individual performance but also cultivates a collective spirit of excellence and innovation. As leaders embody the principles they advocate, they empower others to follow suit, building a legacy of trust, respect, and achievement.

7.5 TURNING CHALLENGES INTO OPPORTUNITIES FOR GROWTH

In leadership, challenges are inevitable, but they are also invaluable. Viewing these challenges as opportunities for growth can transform your leadership style and the overall productivity of your team. Cognitive reframing is a powerful technique to shift your perception of challenges. It involves changing your mindset to see difficulties not as roadblocks, but as stepping stones for development. This approach encourages you to ask, "What can I learn from this?" rather than dwelling on the obstacles. By adopting this mindset, you open yourself to new possibilities and foster an environment where challenges become catalysts for creativity and improvement.

Adversity often spurs innovation. When faced with constraints, teams are forced to think outside the box, leading to creative solutions that might not have emerged otherwise. Consider the case of a tech startup that, during an economic downturn, pivoted its business model to focus on virtual solutions. This shift saved the company and positioned it as a leader in the emerging field of remote work solutions. By embracing adversity as an opportunity for innovation, the startup harnessed the collective creativity of its team, leading to groundbreaking developments that propelled the company forward. These types of examples highlight how challenges can drive innovation when viewed through the lens of possibility.

Fostering a mindset of continuous improvement is essential in transforming challenges into opportunities. This mindset encourages ongoing learning and development, ensuring that your team remains adaptable and forward-thinking. Continuous improvement frameworks, like the Plan-Do-Check-Act cycle, provide a structured approach to implementing changes and evaluating their effectiveness. These frameworks encourage teams to experiment with new ideas, assess their impact, and refine their strategies based on feedback. By promoting a culture of continuous learning, you empower your team to embrace change and view setbacks as opportunities to refine and enhance their skills and processes, creating an environment where growth is a constant pursuit.

Sharing success stories of overcoming obstacles can inspire and motivate your team to see challenges in a new light. Real-life examples of individuals and organizations that have thrived despite adversity provide valuable insights and encouragement. Consider the story of a retail company that faced declining sales due to changing consumer preferences. Instead of succumbing to the pressure, the company reimagined its business model by incorporating digital platforms and personalized shopping experiences. This strategy reversed the downward trend and established the company as a pioneer in the retail industry. By sharing success stories, you demonstrate that challenges can be the springboard for innovation and success, inspiring your team to adopt a similar mindset.

When challenges arise, it's easy to feel overwhelmed and defeated. However, by reframing these challenges as opportunities for growth, you can transform them into powerful drivers of innovation and development. Encourage your team to embrace adversity as a chance to learn and evolve, allowing a culture of continuous improvement and resilience. As you navigate these challenges, remember that each obstacle presents a unique opportunity to strengthen your leadership skills and propel your team toward new heights of success. The path to growth is paved with challenges, and by viewing them through the lens of opportunity, you can lead your team to achieve remarkable outcomes.

7.6 BUILDING EXECUTIVE PRESENCE

Executive presence is a crucial element in effective leadership, serving as the silent yet powerful force that commands attention and respect. It goes beyond mere appearances; it's about the aura of confidence and authority that one exudes. Executive presence comprises key elements such as gravitas, communication skills, and the ability to connect authentically with others. Gravitas involves the ability to project confidence, poise, and decisiveness, particularly in high-pressure situations. It's the calm assurance that others naturally gravitate toward, trusting your leadership even in uncertain times. Strong communication skills are equally important, enabling you to articulate your vision clearly and convincingly. This combination creates a magnetic presence that inspires confidence and motivates others to follow your lead.

Similar to other areas we've discussed, developing communication skills is a vital step in building executive presence too. Both verbal and non-verbal communication play a role in how you are perceived. Public speaking workshops can be invaluable in honing your ability to deliver messages with clarity and impact. These workshops provide a platform to practice speaking in front of an audience, receive constructive feedback, and refine your delivery techniques. Focus on articulation, tone, and pacing to ensure your message is both engaging and effective. Non-verbal communication is equally important; your body language can convey confidence and openness. Techniques such as maintaining eye contact, using purposeful gestures, and adopting an open posture can enhance your presence. These subtle cues reinforce your spoken words, creating a cohesive and compelling communication style.

Cultivating a professional image is another aspect of executive presence that should not be overlooked. Your appearance is often the first impression you make, and it can influence how others perceive your competence and credibility. Professional attire guidelines can help you navigate the nuances of dressing for success. Choose outfits that align with the culture of your organization while reflecting your personal style. A polished appearance extends beyond clothing; grooming and etiquette play a role in how you are perceived. Simple practices such as maintaining neat hair, clean nails, and a professional demeanor contribute to a cohesive image. These details may seem minor, but they contribute to the overall impression of professionalism and attention to detail.

Enhancing decision-making capabilities is essential for those looking to strengthen their executive presence. Decisiveness and strategic thinking are traits that set effective leaders apart. Decision-making models, such as the Six Thinking Hats method, provide structured approaches to evaluating options and making informed choices.

The Six Thinking Hats method was developed by Edward de Bono, where different perspectives and thinking styles are represented by six metaphorical hats. This allows individuals or teams to systematically explore a problem or decision from multiple angles by "putting on" the appropriate hat. Each hat focuses on a specific aspect like facts, emotions, creativity, or critical analysis; essentially promoting parallel thinking and more comprehensive decision-making.

Here are the key attributes of the Six Thinking Hats:

- White Hat: Focuses on facts and information
- Red Hat: Represents emotions and gut feelings
- Black Hat: Critical thinking, identifying potential risks and problems
- Yellow Hat: Optimistic thinking, benefits and positive outcomes
- Green Hat: Creativity, generating new ideas
- Blue Hat: Manages the thinking process, summarizing and organizing

In general, engaging in decision-making exercises can help you practice assessing situations, weighing pros and cons, and arriving at sound conclusions. Confidence in your decision-making abilities fosters trust among your team, reinforcing your role as a capable leader. Clear, well-reasoned decisions demonstrate your ability to navigate complex challenges with poise and assurance.

Receiving and acting on feedback is a critical component of refining executive presence. Feedback loops with leadership coaches or trusted peers can provide insights into how you are perceived by others. Constructive feedback highlights areas for improvement and offers guidance on how to enhance your presence further. Embrace feedback as an opportunity for growth rather than criticism. By actively seeking input and making adjustments, you demonstrate a commitment to continuous improvement. This openness to feedback strengthens your leadership capabilities and sets a positive example for your team, encouraging a culture of learning and development.

Building executive presence is an ongoing process, one that involves self-awareness, practice, and a willingness to evolve. By focusing on communication skills, professional image, decision-making abilities, and feedback, you can cultivate a presence that commands respect and inspires confidence. These elements work in harmony to create a leadership style that is authentic, effective, and impactful. As you develop your executive presence, you enhance your leadership potential and empower those around you to strive for excellence. The journey to building a compelling executive presence is a transformative one, shaping not only your leadership style, but also the way you engage with the world.

BONUS CHAPTER: SKILL #8 - EMPOWERING FUTURE FEMALE LEADERS

Imagine a world where every aspiring female leader has access to the guidance and support needed to reach her full potential. Picture a workplace brimming with diverse voices, each contributing unique perspectives and insights. This vision is more attainable than ever through mentorship and sponsorship, two powerful tools that pave the way for women in leadership.

8.1 EXPLORING VARIOUS WAYS OF MENTORSHIP

As women continue to make strides in the corporate world, the importance of their relationships cannot be overstated. They offer not only guidance, but also a pathway to growth, confidence, and opportunity in environments that have traditionally been male-dominated.

Creating a formal mentorship program is a vital step for organizations committed to encouraging female leadership. These programs connect seasoned leaders with emerging talent, providing a structured environment where knowledge and experience are shared freely. Designing these programs begins with establishing clear frameworks that outline objectives, expectations, and timelines. It's important to set criteria for matching mentors with mentees, ensuring alignment in areas such as career goals, industry experience, and personality traits. For example, a young marketing professional might be paired with a seasoned executive in the same field, allowing for targeted advice and insight into industry-specific challenges. This alignment allows for a relationship where both parties benefit—mentors gain fresh perspectives, while mentees receive the guidance necessary to navigate their career paths.

Sponsorship, on the other hand, takes mentorship a step further by actively advocating for women's career advancement. Sponsors use their influence to open doors and provide opportunities that might otherwise remain out of reach. Effective sponsors possess certain characteristics—they are influential, well-connected, and genuinely invested in the success of their protégés. To identify potential sponsors, women should consider leaders who have the power to affect change within their organizations and who show an interest in supporting emerging talent. Approaching a potential sponsor can be daunting, but it is crucial to be clear about your aspirations and how the sponsor's support could aid in achieving them. Building a relationship based on mutual respect and shared goals lays the foundation for a successful sponsorship.

Informal mentorship opportunities are equally valuable, often providing more flexible and diverse interactions. These connections can be fostered through networking events that focus on mentorship, where conversations naturally lead to mentorship possibilities. Coffee chats and shadowing opportunities offer informal settings to learn from experienced professionals, gaining insights into their day-to-day roles and decision-making processes. These informal relationships can be less intimidating and more adaptable, allowing for spontaneous learning and growth. Encouraging an environment where connections can thrive is essential for any organization committed to developing its female leaders.

Creating mentorship networks amplifies these efforts, offering collective learning and support that extends beyond individual relationships. These networks can be established on platforms that facilitate engagement among mentors and mentees, such as dedicated online forums or professional groups. These spaces provide opportunities for sharing resources, discussing challenges, and celebrating successes. Peer-mentorship initiatives within these networks can further enhance development, as individuals at similar stages in their careers support and learn from one another. Such communities nurture a sense of belonging and empowerment, reinforcing the idea that women are not navigating their leadership journeys alone.

Interactive Element: Designing Your Mentorship Framework

Consider these elements when creating your mentorship program:

- **Objectives**: What are the primary goals of the program? Define clear outcomes for both mentors and mentees.
- **Matching Criteria**: How will you pair mentors with mentees? Consider factors such as career aspirations, expertise, and personality traits.
- **Engagement Platforms**: Which tools or platforms will facilitate communication and interaction? Explore online forums, video conferencing, or in-person meetups.
- **Evaluation Metrics**: What metrics will you use to assess the program's effectiveness? Track progress through regular feedback and performance assessments.

By focusing on these components, you create a dynamic and impactful mentorship program that supports the growth and empowerment of future female leaders.

8.2 SHARING SUCCESS STORIES AND LESSONS LEARNED

Stories possess an unparalleled power to inspire and educate. Facilitating storytelling workshops can serve as a catalyst for personal and professional growth. These workshops encourage leaders to craft impactful narratives, sharing both their successes and the valuable lessons learned from setbacks. The process of articulating one's journey—in all its triumphs and trials—helps leaders connect with their audience on a deeper level. Participants learn to weave their experiences into compelling stories that engage and ignite change. These workshops can include exercises on structuring stories, identifying key themes, and practicing delivery. Storytelling events and panels further provide a platform for these narratives to reach a wider audience, fostering a community of shared wisdom and support.

Highlighting diverse role models within these workshops and events is crucial. By showcasing stories from female leaders across various backgrounds and industries, we provide a tapestry of inspiration. Women who have shattered glass ceilings in fields traditionally dominated by men offer invaluable insights and encouragement. Profiles of these trailblazers reveal the myriad paths to success, emphasizing that leadership is not a one-size-fits-all endeavor. Interviews with these leaders uncover the unique challenges they faced and the strategies they employed to overcome them. Such stories broaden perspectives and affirm the potential within all women to lead, regardless of the barriers they might encounter.

Documenting lessons from failures and challenges is another essential aspect of storytelling. It is through these candid reflections that true learning occurs. Case studies of overcoming failure provide concrete examples of resilience and adaptability, demonstrating that setbacks are not endpoints, but rather opportunities for growth. Reflection exercises encourage leaders to revisit past challenges, examining not only what went wrong, but also what was gained. By normalizing discussions about failure, we create an environment where leaders feel empowered to take risks without fear of judgment.

Promoting storytelling as a learning tool involves more than just sharing experiences; it requires cultivating an environment where these stories can flourish and be dissected for deeper understanding. Storytelling techniques for leadership development focus on extracting and conveying complex lessons in an accessible manner. Leaders can use techniques such as the "hero's journey" framework to map out their experiences, highlighting moments of transformation and growth. Book clubs or discussion groups centered around leadership stories offer a collaborative space for reflection and dialogue. Participants can explore themes and insights from both fictional and real-life narratives, broadening their understanding of leadership dynamics. This collective examination enhances individual growth and strengthens the bonds within the community, as leaders learn from and with each other.

Interactive Element: Crafting Your Leadership Story

Use these prompts to begin crafting your leadership story:

- **Identify a pivotal moment in your career**: What happened, and what was the outcome?
- **Reflect on a failure**: How did it shape your approach to leadership?
- **Consider a lesson learned**: What insights have you gained, and how have they influenced your decisions?

Through these exercises, leaders can articulate their experiences in ways that resonate with others, creating narratives that inspire and guide.

Sharing success stories and lessons learned forms a vital part of leadership development. It encourages reflection, fosters connection, and promotes a culture of continuous learning and growth. In doing so, we empower ourselves and pave the way for future female leaders to rise with confidence and purpose.

8.3 BUILDING LEADERSHIP PIPELINES FOR WOMEN

Identifying high-potential talent within an organization is akin to uncovering hidden gems. It requires a keen eye for recognizing the unique qualities that signal leadership potential. Organizations must employ talent identification and assessment tools to spot these individuals early in their careers. These tools can range from personality assessments that highlight traits like resilience and adaptability, to performance evaluations that focus on problem-solving skills and strategic thinking. Indicators of leadership potential often include a proactive approach to challenges, a knack for inspiring others, and the ability to navigate complex situations with ease. By systematically identifying these traits, companies can nurture future leaders who are ready to step into roles of greater responsibility.

Once high-potential talent is identified, the next step is to develop targeted leadership training programs. These programs should be tailored to meet the specific needs of aspiring female leaders, addressing the unique challenges they face in the workplace. Competency-based training modules can be particularly effective, focusing on areas such as communication skills, decision-making, and emotional intelligence. Leadership workshops that delve into issues like gender bias and work-life balance equip women with the tools they need to succeed. By creating a supportive and enriching environment, organizations can empower women to grow their skills and confidence, preparing them for leadership roles.

Implementing succession planning is crucial for ensuring continuity in leadership and capitalizing on the investment made in developing talent. A well-thought-out succession plan outlines the steps needed to transition individuals into leadership positions, minimizing disruption and maintaining stability. Organizations should begin by identifying key roles within the company and assessing which potential leaders align with these roles. Successful succession programs often include mentorship, job rotation, and leadership development initiatives that prepare individuals for future responsibilities. By establishing clear pathways for advancement, companies secure their leadership future and demonstrate a commitment to employee growth and retention.

Building a culture of growth and development is essential in supporting continuous learning and leadership readiness. This involves creating initiatives that encourage ongoing professional development, such as workshops, seminars, and online courses that keep skills sharp and relevant. Providing learning and career advancement pathways ensures that employees have the resources and support needed to pursue their career goals. Organizations can cultivate an environment where employees are encouraged to seek new challenges, embrace change, and continuously improve. This culture of growth not only benefits individual employees, but also drives innovation and success for the organization as a whole. Cultivating an atmosphere where learning is valued and growth is encouraged can transform an organization into a thriving hub of innovation and leadership excellence.

8.4 ENCOURAGING INTERSECTIONALITY AND DIVERSITY IN LEADERSHIP

Intersectionality is a term that captures the complexity of our identities and how they intersect to shape our experiences, particularly in leadership roles. Coined by Kimberlé Crenshaw, intersectionality acknowledges that people are often disadvantaged by multiple sources of oppression: their race, gender identity, sexual orientation, class, and more. For women in leadership, these intersecting identities can greatly affect their opportunities and experiences. A woman of color, for example, may face challenges that differ significantly from those encountered by a white woman or a man of color. Understanding intersectionality requires recognizing these layered identities and the unique barriers they may impose. It's about seeing beyond a single axis of identity to understand the full picture of a person's lived experience. This perspective is crucial for creating genuinely inclusive and equitable leadership opportunities.

Promoting inclusive leadership practices involves more than acknowledging diversity; it requires active strategies that celebrate and leverage it. One effective approach is to create diverse leadership teams that reflect a variety of backgrounds and perspectives. These teams are better equipped to address the complexities of an increasingly global and multicultural marketplace. Policies supporting intersectional representation ensure that decisions are informed by a broad spectrum of experiences and ideas. For instance, implementing recruitment strategies that target underrepresented groups can help build teams that are not only diverse, but also more resilient and innovative. These strategies include using unbiased recruitment tools and fostering an inclusive culture where all voices are heard and valued. By creating environments where diverse identities are not just present but are actively shaping the direction of the organization, leaders can drive meaningful change.

Systemic barriers to diversity in leadership are often deeply entrenched, requiring deliberate efforts to dismantle them. These barriers can include biases in hiring practices, a lack of mentorship opportunities for women of color, and corporate cultures that favor homogeneity. Studies on these systemic barriers reveal that they are pervasive across industries, often operating unconsciously yet influencing decisions and policies. Organizations can implement initiatives to break down these barriers, such as diversity training programs that focus on recognizing and overcoming implicit biases.

Encouraging open forums for discussion and implementing mentorship programs specifically for intersectional leaders can also make a significant impact. By addressing these barriers head-on, companies improve diversity and enhance their overall performance, as diverse teams have been shown to be more innovative and effective.

Celebrating diverse leadership contributions is vital for reinforcing the value of intersectional identities in leadership. Recognizing the achievements of leaders from varied backgrounds honors their efforts and sets a precedent for what is possible. Diversity awards and recognition programs can spotlight these leaders, showcasing their successes and encouraging others to follow in their footsteps. Publicizing stories of diverse leaders, whether through company newsletters, social media, or industry publications, serves to inspire and motivate. These stories offer proof that diverse leadership is not only achievable but beneficial, enriching the organizational culture and contributing to a more inclusive environment. Celebrating such contributions helps to shift narratives, fostering a culture where diverse identities are seen as assets that enhance leadership effectiveness and organizational success.

8.5 LEADING WITH IMPACT AND PURPOSE

To lead with impact, it's crucial to understand your personal leadership purpose. This purpose serves as your guiding star, influencing every decision and action you take. It's not just about knowing what you want to achieve, but understanding why it matters. Start by reflecting on what truly drives you. What are the values and passions that fuel your ambition? Consider purpose statement exercises to help articulate these thoughts. Write down what you stand for and how you wish to impact those around you. Through reflection prompts, explore questions like, "What legacy do I want to leave?" or "What are the causes I am most passionate about?" These reflections help distill your motivations into a clear, actionable purpose that aligns with your leadership style.

Aligning your personal leadership purpose with your organization's mission ensures that your actions support broader goals. This alignment is vital for creating coherence and unity within a team. Consider how your purpose complements the organization's vision. Are there areas where your goals intersect? Case studies of mission-aligned leadership reveal how leaders effectively integrate their personal values with organizational objectives, creating synergy and driving success. Strategies for communicating purpose to your team involve transparency and storytelling. Share your vision and how it ties into the larger mission. Encourage open dialogue, allowing team members to express how their roles contribute to achieving these shared objectives.

Measuring and evaluating your leadership impact requires a thoughtful approach. It's about understanding the tangible and intangible effects of your leadership on both your team and organization. Utilize impact measurement frameworks to assess areas such as team performance, employee satisfaction, and goal achievement. These frameworks help identify strengths and areas for improvement, guiding your development as a leader. Establish feedback loops to ensure continuous improvement. Regularly seek input from your team, peers, and supervisors. This feedback not only highlights areas for growth but also reinforces what is working well. By actively engaging in this process, you demonstrate a commitment to excellence and adaptability, setting a standard for others to follow.

Leading with purpose naturally inspires and motivates those around you. Purpose-driven leaders like Indra Nooyi and Oprah Winfrey illustrate how a strong sense of purpose can transform a vision into reality. Their leadership styles are marked by clarity, passion, and authenticity, which resonate deeply with their teams and audiences. Techniques for communicating vision and impact include storytelling, where you share personal experiences that underline your purpose. Use visual aids, such as infographics or presentations, to illustrate your goals and progress. Encourage your team to contribute their ideas and insights, fostering a collaborative environment where everyone feels heard and valued. This inclusive approach strengthens your leadership impact and empowers others to embrace their purpose and contribute to shared success.

As we reflect on the journey of empowering future female leaders, it becomes clear that leading with impact and purpose is more than a leadership style. It's a way of being that connects deeply with the core values of authenticity, inclusivity, and growth. By aligning personal purpose with organizational goals, measuring impact, and inspiring through purposeful leadership, we pave the way for a future where diverse voices and perspectives thrive. This chapter emphasizes the profound influence of purpose-driven leadership in transforming not only teams and organizations but also the broader landscape of female leadership.

HELP OTHERS TRANSLATE THEIR VISION INTO REALITY

Leadership is undoubtedly one of the greatest and most fulfilling challenges you will take on in your life. Few other life tasks necessitate such keen self-awareness and communication abilities. As a true leader, you not only set goals, determine roles and processes... you create an entire culture. You connect with others on a profound level, inspiring them to produce their best results while also achieving a sense of personal fulfillment.

If this book has demonstrated a thorough roadmap to becoming an effective and inspirational female leader, kindly share your opinion with other readers.

I wish you the sense of joy, pride, and satisfaction that arises when you serve as the guide who enables so many people to achieve their personal best.

Click here to leave your review on Amazon.

https://www.amazon.com/review/create-review/?asin=B0F1G476KF

CONCLUSION

In this journey together, we have explored the world of female leadership, focusing on embracing authenticity, overcoming challenges, and leading with impact, especially in environments where women often find themselves as pioneers. The central theme of this book is empowerment—empowering you to bring your authentic self to the forefront, to navigate the complexities of leadership with confidence, and to leave a lasting impact.

Throughout the chapters, we delved into seven essential skills crucial for female leaders. First, discovering your authentic leadership style is about understanding your core values and strengths. It's about leading from a place of truth and integrity. Next, we tackled overcoming imposter syndrome, a barrier many women face. By identifying triggers and reframing self-perception, you can build resilience against self-doubt.

We also examined navigating gender bias and stereotypes, skills crucial for breaking barriers in male-dominated spaces. Recognizing and addressing subtle biases helps you create a more inclusive environment. Building a supportive network was another key skill, emphasizing the importance of connections and mentorship in your leadership journey.

Establishing psychological safety within teams is vital for fostering innovation and trust. When team members feel safe, they are more likely to contribute openly and creatively. Balancing professional and personal life is a challenge many leaders face. Implementing strategies for effective time management and self-care ensures you maintain your well-being while achieving professional success. Finally, developing a dynamic leadership style involves embracing flexibility and adaptability, allowing you to navigate change with confidence.

As we reflect on these skills, I encourage you to consider the insights and strategies shared throughout this book. These practical applications are designed to enhance your leadership journey, providing tools to navigate challenges and seize opportunities. Whether it's through journaling exercises, role-playing scenarios, or networking strategies, these skills offer tangible benefits for your growth as a leader.

Reflecting on my own journey, I have learned that leadership is not a destination but a continuous path of growth and discovery. Each challenge faced and each success celebrated has shaped my leadership style, teaching me the value of authenticity, resilience, and community. These lessons have reinforced the importance of staying true to oneself while embracing the diverse perspectives that enrich our leadership experiences.

I invite you to take the skills and strategies discussed and apply them to your leadership journey. Identify your authentic leadership style, build a network of support, and foster an environment of psychological safety within your teams. These actions will not only empower you, but also create a positive impact on those around you.

Embrace challenges as opportunities for growth and innovation. Engage in continuous learning, seeking new knowledge and experiences that expand your horizons. As you grow, consider the impact you can have on others. Become a mentor and support other women in their leadership journeys. By doing so, you contribute to a ripple effect of empowerment and inclusivity in your organizations and communities.

As we conclude this exploration, I want to leave you with an inspirational message. Embrace your unique qualities and lead with authenticity, confidence, and purpose. Your potential to make a lasting impact is immense. By staying true to yourself and supporting others, you can transform the landscape of leadership for future generations. Believe in your abilities, take bold steps forward, and inspire those around you with your vision and courage. The world needs your leadership, so go forth and lead with impact!

REFERENCES

- Forbes Business Council. (2022, March 10). *Eight powerful examples of women in leadership (and what we can all learn from them)*. Forbes. https://www.forbes.com/councils/forbesbusinesscouncil/2022/03/10/eight-powerful-examples-of-women-leadership-and-what-we-can-all-learn-from-them/
- Cecchi-Dimeglio, P. (2024, February 14). *How self-awareness elevates leadership effectiveness*. Forbes. https://www.forbes.com/sites/paolacecchi-dimeglio/2024/02/14/how-self-awareness-elevates-leadership-effectiveness/
- Forbes Technology Council. (2023, November 16). *Empathy in leadership: The powerful balance of strength and compassion*. Forbes. https://www.forbes.com/councils/forbestechcouncil/2023/11/16/empathy-in-leadership-the-powerful-balance-of-strength-and-compassion/
- Harvard Kennedy School Case Program. (2017, September 19). *The life and legacy of Nelson Mandela*. https://case.hks.harvard.edu/values-based-leadership-across-difference-the-life-and-legacy-of-nelson-mandela/
- Bravata, D. M., Madhusudhan, D. K., & Bhasin, M. (2023). *Imposter phenomenon*. StatPearls. National Center for Biotechnology Information. https://www.ncbi.nlm.nih.gov/books/NBK585058/
- Ackerman, C. E. (2023). *30 best journaling prompts for improving mental health*. Positive Psychology. https://positivepsychology.com/journaling-prompts/
- TalentLMS. (2024, October 10). *8 growth mindset examples and ways to develop it*. https://www.talentlms.com/blog/growth-mindset-examples/
- Her New Standard. (n.d.). *Overcoming imposter syndrome: Advice from women leaders*. https://hernewstandard.com/imposter-syndrome-tips-women-leaders/
- Lean In. (2023). *Women in the workplace 2023: The full digital report*. https://leanin.org/women-in-the-workplace/2023
- Healthline. (2023, October 18). *Microaggressions in the workplace: Examples and solutions*. https://www.healthline.com/health/microaggressions-in-the-workplace
- Harvard Division of Continuing Education. (n.d.). *Emotional intelligence in leadership training program*. https://professional.dce.harvard.edu/programs/emotional-intelligence-in-leadership/

REFERENCES

- Diversity Social. (2023, July 4). *The power of allyship in the workplace: An expert's overview.* https://diversity.social/allyship-in-the-workplace-experts/
- Cross, R. (2020). *The secrets of successful female networkers.* Harvard Business Review. https://www.robcross.org/wp-content/uploads/2020/05/HBR-The-secrets-of-successful-female-networkers.pdf
- Committee of 200. (2021, October 26). *Mentoring matters: The importance of female mentorship.* Forbes. https://www.forbes.com/sites/committeeof200/2021/10/26/mentoring-matters-the-importance--of-female-mentorship/
- Cake. (2024, May 17). *10 best professional networking sites to expand your connections.* https://www.cake.me/resources/best-professional-networking-sites?locale=en
- Harvard Business Review. (2024, March). *Research: How women can build high-status networks.* https://hbr.org/2024/03/research-how-women-can-build-high-status-networks
- Forbes Business Council. (2022, October 12). *Psychological safety: Building high-performing teams.* Forbes. https://www.forbes.com/councils/forbesbusinesscouncil/2022/10/12/psychological-safety-building-high-performing-teams/
- Forbes Coaches Council. (2023, May 31). *20 smart ways managers can foster more open dialogue in the workplace.* Forbes. https://www.forbes.com/councils/forbescoachescouncil/2023/05/31/20-smart-ways-managers-can-foster-more-open-dialogue-in-the-workplace/
- Forbes Business Council. (2023, August 16). *The power of diversity and inclusion: Driving innovation and success.* Forbes. https://www.forbes.com/councils/forbesbusinesscouncil/2023/08/16/the-power-of-diversity-and-inclusion-driving-innovation-and-success/
- Harvard Business Review. (2024, January). *How high-performing teams build trust.* https://hbr.org/2024/01/how-high-performing-teams-build-trust
- Asana. (2025, January 29). *The Eisenhower Matrix: How to prioritize your to-do list.* https://asana.com/resources/eisenhower-matrix#:~:text=The%20Eisenhower%20Matrix%20is%20a,the%20tasks%20you'll%20delete.
- Todoist. (n.d.). *Time blocking—Your complete guide to more focused work.* https://todoist.com/productivity-methods/time-blocking
- Mayo Clinic. (2023, November 30). *Job burnout: How to spot it and take action.* https://www.mayoclinic.org/healthy-lifestyle/adult-health/in-depth/burnout/art-20046642
- Sargent, J. (2023, June 23). *Work, life, and everything in between: The power of mindset.* LinkedIn. https://www.linkedin.com/pulse/work-life-everything-between-power-mindset-jan-sargent

REFERENCES

- MIT Career Development Office. (2023, September 14). *10 most common leadership styles and their pros and cons.* https://cdo.mit.edu/blog/2023/09/14/10-most-common-leadership-styles-and-their-pros-and-cons-in-2023/
- Maxwell Leadership. (2024, August 27). *5 strategies for women to build resilience.* https://www.maxwellleadership.com/blog/strategies-women-leaders-resilience-tenacity/
- Harvard Business Review. (2024, January). *The new rules of executive presence.* https://hbr.org/2024/01/the-new-rules-of-executive-presence
- The Collective. (2023, May 24). *Adaptive leadership: Driving change with real examples.* https://www.jointhecollective.com/article/adaptive-leadership-driving-change-with-real-examples/
- Bay Path University. (2023, December 11). *7 valuable women-led mentorships for development.* https://online.baypath.edu/resources/article/value-of-women-led-mentorships/
- MindTools. (n.d.). *The power of storytelling in female leadership.* https://www.mindtools.com/alasqjt/the-power-of-storytelling-in-female-leadership#:~:text=A%20great%20example%20of%20effective,her%20storytelling%2C%20built%20strong%20bonds.
- Forbes Human Resources Council. (2023, November 16). *20 ways leaders can improve workplace diversity, equity, and inclusion.* Forbes. https://www.forbes.com/councils/forbeshumanresourcescouncil/2023/11/16/20-ways-leaders-can-improve-on-workplace-diversity-equity-and-inclusion/
- Haslam College of Business. (2023, August 21). *Understanding the role of intersectionality in the workplace.* https://haslam.utk.edu/news/understanding-the-role-of-intersectionality-in-the-workplace/

www.ingramcontent.com/pod-product-compliance
Lightning Source LLC
Chambersburg PA
CBHW071711210326
41597CB00017B/2440